P9-BJS-321

A Practical Handbook for parents of children
with congenital heart problems

This book is especially dedicated to Robert and Jessica
of New Zealand

and to Heart Children and
their parents everywhere

Published by
Heart Line Association
c/o Sun Microsystems Ltd, Watchmoor Park, Riverside Way, Camberley
Surrey, GU15 3YL
'Heart Children: A Practical Handbook for Parents' 2 r.e. (Pbk)
ISBN 0 9515270 10
© 1989 Heart Line Association

1st printed September 1989 (6M)
2nd Edition January 1992 (20M)

Written by Philip G. Rees, Adelaide M. Tunstill, Tricia Pope,
David Kinnear and Susan Rees

Artwork and typesetting by The FD Group Limited, Fleet, Hants
Printed by Rapid Print, Houghton Regis, Beds
Heart Line Association is a registered charity, number 295803

FOREWORD
Making sense of it all

The purpose of this book is to help you deal with some of the feelings and problems that come your way as you live with a child who has a heart problem.

You may be familiar with these feelings already — in which case you have trodden the same path as the parents who contributed to this book. You may have experienced with us the struggle to try and make sense of it all.

You will have learned that each child's condition is different from any other. That some conditions are minor while others cannot be corrected. Some children die while others with similar conditions live.

You will become aware, if you are not already, that there are no stock answers to guide you through the difficult times. We hope we can help you to come to terms with your feelings and channel them positively as you move through all the emotions and experiences that your child will bring you. We hope this book will help you to be able to cope with — and actually enjoy your life with your child who has a heart problem.

GENERAL

The majority of children with heart disease in developed countries have what is called congenital heart disease, that is, their hearts have developed abnormally early on in pregnancy. One in one hundred and twenty-five of all children born in Britain have this form of heart problem. Some may be very minor and never require treatment, others may be mild and need occasional follow-up, others may be serious, requiring major operations, and a few are so serious that no treatment is currently available. The possibility of treatment has improved enormously over the past fifteen years, and the majority of children, even those with very serious problems, can now be treated very successfully.

Sometimes a previously normal heart can be affected by inflammation or infection, although that subject is outside the scope of this book, except where it relates to congenital heart problems.

ABOUT THE WRITERS

Heart Children has been written by a group of five people who have practical experience on the subject from first hand knowledge:

Philip Rees is Consultant Pediatric Cardiologist at The Hospital for Sick Children, Great Ormond Street, London – and well known by very many parents.

Adelaide Tunstill is also at The Hospital for Sick Children – where she is Clinical Nursing Officer in charge of the Cardiac Wing – and is universally acknowledged for her experience and expertise in the subject by both doctors, nurses and parents.

Tricia Pope is a former Chairman of Heart Line Association, teaches Psychology – and first had the idea of preparing this book. Tricia's son Simon, has a Congenital Heart Disorder.

David Kinnear who also published this book, was the first parent Chairman of Heart Line Association, and has two daughters, Emma and Annabel, who were both born with severe heart problems.

Sue Rees, former Social Worker at the Brompton Hospital, London, has wide experience of working with children who have Congenital Heart Disorders and their parents.

ABOUT THIS BOOK

This book is written both for the parents of children with heart disease – and for the children and adolescents themselves.

The impetus to prepare it came from seeing **Linda Davies** and **Michelle Mann's** lucid 'Heart Children' booklet from New Zealand.

Further encouragement came from the **Danish Heart Foundation** booklet, 'Congenital Heart Defects' – and also from the excellent handouts that **Doctors Olive Scott** and **Leon Gerlis** and the British Heart Foundation had prepared over the past few years.

We have used the term 'Heart Child' for convenience as many of us parents do. This does not mean to belittle or diminish in any way our child as an individual who happens to have a heart abnormality. Our aim is for our children to grow up as normally as possible. We have also used 'he' and 'him' rather than both 'he' and 'she', again for convenience. These terms can be replaced by 'she' and 'her'.

The book is designed to improve knowledge and understanding. It is an outline and many generalisations have had to be made. It in NO WAY replaces personal contact between the family and the teams involved in your child's care. PLEASE ASK QUESTIONS of the team looking after your child – so that problems and plans are understood. There are many grey zones in medicine in which the decisions made concerning your child and the actions taken may not follow the outline of this book, so do not be alarmed if what you read here differs from your own experience.

PUBLISHER'S STATEMENT

Contents

1 THE NORMAL HEART
Its circulation and development

The heart is a pump with four chambers within it; the two (left and right) atria, and the two (left and right) ventricles. Its purpose is to pump blood that has been to the body, and given up its oxygen to the various organs, into the lungs to pick up oxygen, and then to return that oxygenated blood into the body to supply the organs with oxygen and nutrition.

Blood returns from the body in veins and the veins join together to form two large veins, one from the top half of the body (the superior vena cava), and one from the bottom half of the body (the inferior vena cava) which run into the

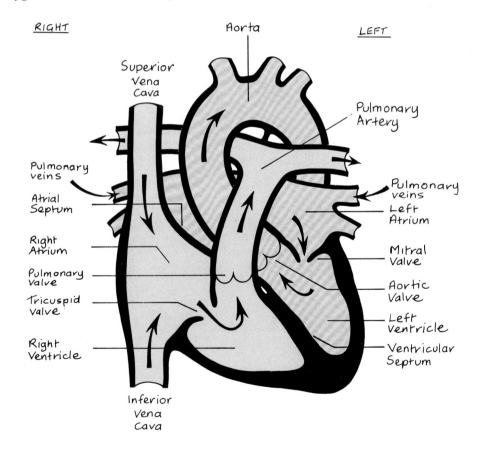

RIGHT   Aorta   LEFT

Superior Vena Cava

Pulmonary Artery

Pulmonary veins

Atrial Septum

Pulmonary veins

Left Atrium

Right Atrium

Mitral Valve

Pulmonary valve

Aortic Valve

Tricuspid valve

Left Ventricle

Right Ventricle

Ventricular Septum

Inferior Vena Cava

NORMAL CIRCULATION

first chamber of the heart (the right atrium). This acts as a reservoir to fill the right ventricle which it does through a flap valve (the tricuspid valve). When the right ventricle contracts, this flap valve closes, the pressure in the pump chamber rises above that in the lung artery, and the pulmonary valve opens. Blood is then pumped into the lung artery and both lungs. When the ventricle starts to relax, the lung (pulmonary) valve closes which stops blood leaking back into the ventricle.

Within the lungs the main arteries branch into very many small vessels which have thinner and thinner walls. They run very close to the end of the airway passages, and at this point oxygen is taken up from the air and carbon dioxide is given off into the air passages. The blood then returns from the lungs in veins which join together, the four of these entering the receiving chamber on the left side of the heart (the left atrium). This acts as a reservoir to fill the left ventricle through another flap valve (the mitral valve). This ventricle then contracts, closing the flap valve, the pressure rises, the aortic valve opens between the left ventricle and the aorta and blood is pumped out into the aorta. This is the large vessel that arises from the heart, divides into many vessels that supply the whole of the body. Following this, the ventricle relaxes and the aortic valve closes. During relaxation of the ventricles the mitral and tricuspid valves open, and blood flows into them in preparation for the next contraction.

This process of contraction followed by relaxation occurs between 70-150 times per minute depending on the age of the patient. The heart's electrical circuit, the conducting system, controls this rate and ensures that the atria contract just before the ventricles. The heart's own spontaneous pacemaker (the sinus node) is at the top right hand corner of the right atrium. It generates an electrical impulse. This impulse (similar to what happens in a nerve) spreads through the atria causing them to contract. It then reaches the junction between the atria and the right ventricle at the atrioventricular node. There, after a short delay, the electrical signal is passed down very fast conducting fibres into both ventricles which causes them to contract.

The lungs are relatively small and have fewer and thinner walled blood vessels in comparison to those in the body. It is relatively easier for blood to be pumped through them. The pressures thus generated in the right side of the heart are much less, usually a quarter, of those required by the left side of the heart to pump blood all around the body. The normal left ventricle is therefore thick, and the normal right ventricle is thin. Both atria are thin walled, acting largely as reservoirs and only having to contract to fill the relaxed ventricles.

The heart muscle itself receives its blood supply from the coronary arteries which arise from the bottom of the aorta. These vessels are usually normal in children but are damaged in later life by smoking, high blood pressure, obesity and high fat diets.

Heart Development

The heart develops from a small group of cells in the upper part of the chest of the very small embryo. These cells rapidly form a tube and the tube folds over on itself into an 'S' shape. Bulges develop on this tube and these form the chambers of the heart and the first part of the major arteries. Between these bulges are waists. It is here that the valves develop. The heart is divided into left and right sides by walls or septae, these grow between the two atria, the two ventricles, and also separate the two arteries.

The heart connects up with the simultaneously developing blood vessels in the body, and those within the lungs. This process is complete by ten weeks of pregnancy, following which the heart and the blood vessels just grow with the developing baby.

Circulation before birth

Before birth the placenta (after-birth) is the organ that supplies the baby with oxygen and nutrition, and removes carbon dioxide. The lungs are not expanded and require only a small blood supply to allow them to grow. Nature has devised several short circuits to allow the most efficient use of blood flow whilst in the womb. The oxygenated blood from the placenta returns to the inferior vena cava in the umbilical vein, and then is directed by a flap valve (Eustachian valve) towards the small hole (foramen ovale) between the two receiving chambers. This oxygenated blood is then pumped by the left ventricle into the aorta and up to the developing brain.

The de-oxygenated blood from the top half of the body is directed to the right ventricle which pumps it into the lung artery. The majority of the blood then goes into a tube (the ductus) down the aorta into the abdomen from where the arteries arise that feed the placenta.

It is because of these connections and with the placenta in the circuit, that the majority of babies even with very major heart problems will often be apparently fine and grow normally within the womb.

Changes at birth and within the subsequent few days

The placenta is removed from the circulation as soon as the umbilical cord is clamped. The lungs expand with crying and blood passes into them in increasing amounts. This blood picks up the oxygen from the air, and the increased amount of blood returning to the left atrium closes the flap valve between the two atria.

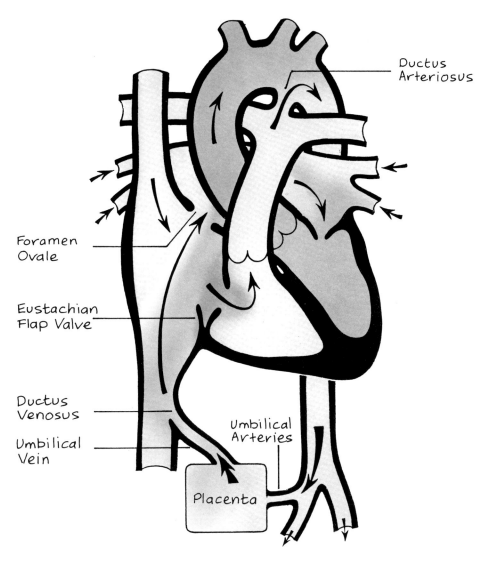

Ductus Arteriosus

Foramen Ovale

Eustachian Flap Valve

Ductus Venosus

Umbilical Vein

Umbilical Arteries

Placenta

CIRCULATION BEFORE BIRTH

Over the next few days, the tube between the two arteries gradually closes. These changes result in an increased amount of oxygen being available to the child as a result of the lungs working. The blood pressure in the body increases, and gradually over the subsequent days and weeks, that in the lungs and in the right ventricle, falls.

Babies with significant heart problems may first show something abnormal when these changes in the circulation occur.

2 FINDING OUT WHAT'S WRONG
Examinations and Investigations

The general practitioner, paediatrician or cardiologist will examine your child. They will look at his size, height and weight, the colour of lips, tongue and fingers, and the shape of his nails, which may be abnormal (clubbing). They will count the child's pulse and assess its quality in the arms and the legs, and often they will measure the blood pressure. They will feel the child's abdomen to look for the size of the liver, look at the chest shape and feel the heart's action. Then with their stethoscopes they will listen to the heart sounds, and also any murmurs. Heart sounds are the noises produced as the heart valves close, and murmurs are produced by the flow of blood through the heart and large vessels.

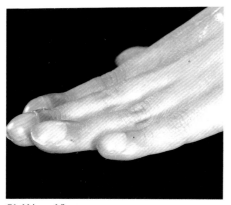

Clubbing of fingers

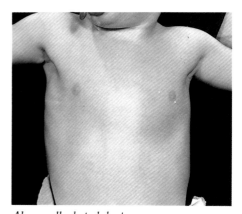

Abnormally shaped chest

1 MURMURS

Murmurs are most frequently entirely normal coming from the normal blood flow. These are termed innocent and all is well. Other murmurs come from abnormal blood flows and may be the only sign of a problem being present. They are often picked up during a routine examination or an incidental illness.

2 BREATHLESSNESS

Children with heart problems become breathless sooner than ordinary children. This occurs either because of too much or too little blood in the lungs. If too much, the lungs are heavier than normal. More effort and energy is used to expand them to move air in and out. In small children this breathlessness causes poor feeding, slow weight gain and sweating. In older children it reduces exercise tolerance.

If too little blood goes to the lungs, not enough oxygen can be picked up to meet the increasing needs of the body muscles on exercise. This lack of oxygen causes an increase in the rate and depth of breathing.

3 BLUENESS

Blueness of fingers and lips can be a normal finding in children, and relates to alterations in size of the fine blood vessels of the skin and is often caused by temperature changes. Blueness of the tongue as well as fingers and toes occurs if darker blood, with less oxygen, has been pumped into the body, without first passing through the lungs.

4 DIZZINESS/FAINTING

This may relate to alterations in the heart rate or to obstruction in the blood flow from the heart into the great arteries.

5 FATIGUE

Children who are blue, or whose heart muscle is working poorly, may complain of tiredness and lack of energy. This is because the muscles of the legs and arms are not receiving enough oxygenated blood.

6 SPELLS

If the muscle below the lung artery becomes thickened, it can reduce the blood flow to the lungs. The extent of the narrowing can change – when it is tight the blood flow to the lungs falls temporarily. The amount of oxygenated blood available to the body is reduced and the child becomes bluer. This can come on suddenly without apparent reason, often after breakfast. It is associated with a funny cry – as though in distress – restlessness, breathing difficulties followed by exhaustion and floppiness and it is termed a 'Spell'. These 'Spells' are usually mild to start with and settle on their own. Over time they can become longer lasting and more serious, and it is important that your doctors are told about them.

7 SQUATTING

Blue children often squat on their haunches after walking or running. It is a normal response and increases the blood flow to the lungs by raising the blood pressure. Therefore more oxygenated blood is available and the children feel better and their colour improves.

8 CHEST PAIN

This is very unusual in children with heart problems, and rarely comes from the heart itself but from muscles in the chest.

9 SUDDEN COLLAPSE

This also is very unusual in children's heart problems, and the vast majority of families can be reassured that this will not happen.

10 PALPITATIONS

This is the sensation of the heart beating heavily or quickly. Minor sensations are entirely normal as are extra beats. Fast heart beating, similar to the usual fast heart beat on running, may come on suddenly at rest. Usually these are a nuisance and frequently children learn special tricks to slow the heart rate. Occasionally the fast heart beat lasts for a long time causing sweatiness, paleness, breathlessness and may require specific treatment.

Investigations – the way to discover what needs to be done

Frequently, investigations are necessary to help find the exact type of heart problem that is present. Not all children will require all, or even any, of the tests. The decision will depend on each individual child.

ELECTROCARDIOGRAM (ECG)

The ECG records the faint electrical impulses which arise from the electrical circuits within the heart. It is recorded by wires and plates or sticky patches connected to the child's arms, legs and chest. The recording is painless and takes about five minutes. It shows the heart rhythm and also may help in assessing which chambers are performing extra work.

TWENTY-FOUR HOUR ECG RECORDING

This is a recording of the electrical activity over a twenty-four hour period, using a small tape-recorder and wires attached to the chest. It can be undertaken as an Out-patient, with the child doing normal things during the day, except bathing, swimming or playing in a sandpit. This is often used when children have symptoms of fainting, dizziness or irregularities of their heart beat.

CHEST X-RAY

Chest X-ray shows the size and site of the heart and gives an assessment of blood flow through the lungs. It may also show which part of the heart is enlarged.

By combining the ECG and the chest X-ray, often a very accurate diagnosis can be made.

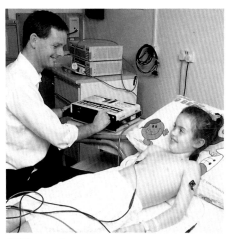

ECG recording

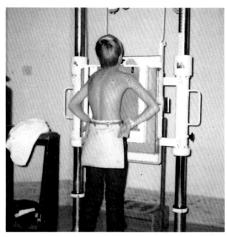

Chest X-ray

Echocardiography

This uses very high pitched sound waves (sonar) to see the heart structure and assess its function. The test is painless, although some of the little children get rather restless during it and may require to be sedated. The probe, which generates the sound wave, is placed on the chest, the top of the abdomen and the neck. The sound beam is reflected back to the probe which is connected to a computer and then to a television screen. The pictures of the heart and its blood vessels can be seen and recorded. This may be done as an Out-patient and takes between fifteen minutes to an hour depending on the complexity of the problem.

The noise of the blood flow can be magnified producing a 'whooshing' sound. This is known as the 'doppler' test and has become very useful particularly in assessing narrrowings in the circulation.

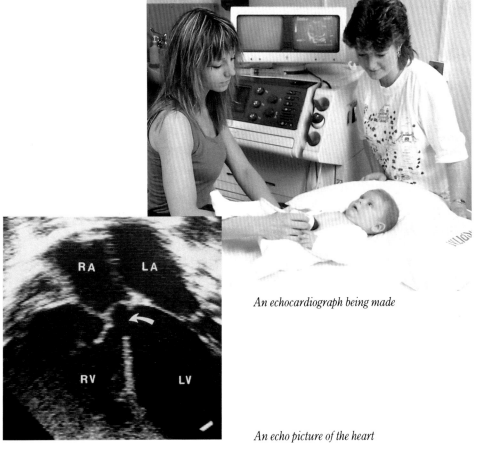

An echocardiograph being made

An echo picture of the heart

Cardiac Catheterization and Angiography

This involves the child coming into hospital for about three days. The first day is to help the child get used to everyone and to have an X-ray and ECG. Sedatives are often given that night as well as just before the test the following day. The patient may not eat or drink for about four hours before the procedure starts. A nurse who knows the child will bring him to the Catheter Room. The little children are carried and the bigger ones travel on a trolley. The child lies quietly on a flat table connected to an ECG machine, and there are X-ray machines which allow the heart's action to be filmed. The doctors and nurses wear special trousers, shirts, hats, gloves and put on masks to keep clean.

In some hospitals this test is done under local anaesthesia and sedation, and in others under general anaesthesia. If the former, the local anaesthetic is put into the area where the tube is to be inserted. This is usually the top of the leg or occasionally the arms. Then either through a needle, or in some children with a small incision, the catheter (small tube) is inserted into the vein and/or artery. By gently manipulating the catheter it moves along with the blood flow through the big blood vessels and the various chambers of the heart. This enables the pressures to be measured within each chamber and the various arteries, and also small samples of blood are taken from each part of the circulation. This shows whether there are any significant holes between the different parts of the system, and which chambers are working abnormally. A liquid can also be injected down these tubes which is visible on the X-ray screen and this will show us the heart structure, any abnormality and the heart's function.

Recently this test has been used to treat heart problems e.g. stretching narrow valves, and operations may thus be avoided.

The test takes between one and three hours depending on the complexity of the case and following this the child will

The catheter room

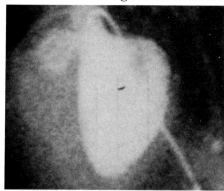

An angiocardiogram — The white line is the catheter

14

be sleepy for a few hours, and then return to normal. Usually the child is well enough to return home the next day.

Although this test is a complex one, it can, in the vast majority of children, be performed very safely without problems.

Other techniques

RADIO-ISOTOPE SCANNING
An injection of a very small dose of an isotope can be used either to assess the function of heart muscle or the extra amount of blood going through lungs in children who have holes between the two sides of the circulation. This can be done as an Out-patient with a small injection and the child just has to lie still on an X-ray table for a short period of time.

ELECTROPHYSIOLOGICAL STUDIES
Occasionally in children who have repeated problems from abnormalities of the heart rate and rhythm, more detailed investigations are required with regards to the electrical circuitry. This involves putting several small, fine catheters into different parts of the circulation and recording the electrical activity directly from the inside of the heart. In addition, the different areas of the heart can be stimulated by these catheters to assess the electrical abnormality. This test is very similar to the catheter test, and therefore involves admission to hospital for several days.

BARIUM SWALLOW
The child's oesophagus (gullet) can be seen on a television picture and X-rays taken while taking milk containing barium. If there is any narrowing of the oesophagus or main windpipe (the trachea) caused by an abnormal blood vessel, this can usually be seen clearly with this test.

NUCLEAR MAGNETIC RESONANCE (NMR)
This involves placing the child in a strong variable magnetic field. Images are produced looking at the alteration of electrical forces in different parts of the body. It is possible to see structures extremely clearly and to measure blood flow very accurately. It involves lying still in an enclosed space, rather like a torpedo tube, for a long time, and is usually done under full anaesthesia in children.

HAEMOGLOBIN
This is the chemical in the red blood cells that carries oxygen and carbon dioxide around the body. The amount present can be easily measured by a simple blood test. It is useful to check this occasionally to ensure that the level is correct, not too low, not too high for the child's condition. In blue children the level is usually higher than normal which is an advantage. However the level should not be allowed to become too high as the blood is then very thick and flows sluggishly. When this happens, operations may be advised even if the child is otherwise well. If operations are not possible some of the thick blood may be removed and replaced by a salt solution in order to dilute it.

OXYGEN SATURATION
The percentage of haemoglobin that is carrying oxygen to the tissues of the body can be measured directly with a simple probe that is attached to a finger or an ear lobe. This is a painless, simple and reliable test.

3 REACTIONS
Your feelings and those around you

DISCOVERY

When parents are expecting the birth of a child there is a great feeling of excitement and elation, new hopes for the future, joy and anticipation. But behind these happy feelings, there is a dark shadow. What if there is something wrong with our baby? Most people put this thought out of their heads, so it is a terrible shock to most of us when we learn our child has a heart condition.

When this happens to us — and our child — it is difficult to accept. 'Why me?' you may ask, a question which we assure you, has no answer yet.

SORROW

When you discover you have a child with a heart problem it would be unusual not to feel deep unhappiness. The natural way the body copes with this is through tears — a good way to release the pent-up emotions of sorrow and despair. You may try to hold back your tears for fear of embarrassing others — or because you think you may not be able to stop. But don't be. It is not only acceptable but good to share your sorrow, and you will probably feel better for it. A word for fathers, here. Unfortunately the idea of men crying in our western society has in some way become taboo. You are meant to keep a 'stiff upper lip', come what may. This is a pity because it denies you one of nature's ways of coping with your agony. So take our advice, find a quiet corner and let it all go. You will feel better able to cope after — and you will be more able to support your partners.

ANGER

Anger is another emotion you may need to deal with. It is natural to want to 'lash out' at others when we feel hurt or cornered. If you have a faith, you may feel angry with God for letting it happen to you. Parents are often angry with themselves, because they think they have damaged their child and they feel guilty.

At times you will feel anger with almost everybody else. Most parents deny their feelings of anger — but it is very, very natural.

It is all right to feel angry at this time. Try and talk it out with caring friends.

SHOCK

Initially, when you first discover your child has a problem you may have overwhelming feelings of panic and despair, and then a kind of numbness. This is your mind's way of protecting you and allowing in only the amount of pain and upset you can handle.

This book is written by parents who have experienced this trauma — we can tell you that it is a NORMAL HEALTHY RESPONSE.

As the shock fades you may experience other feelings
— as if you are living in a bad dream
— you may become forgetful, unable to concentrate (especially problematic for parents at work)
— making decisions may be difficult, because you cannot anticipate the future.

DEPRESSION AND ANXIETY

Experiences of parents of heart children indicate that we all go through a see-saw world of elation as some new good information arrives, only to end up in anxiety and depression as things get worse, perhaps as a result of a chance remark from a member of the medical staff — or the effect of some treatment or other. Then there is an improvement — and, up we go again! Waiting for results of tests — the time before an operation — the wait when it is actually happening — all can be very frightening times.

This 'see saw' of emotions may cause you desperate fatigue, depression and even despair. But you can and will be able to come to terms with it. The key is to keep talking to people who know what you are going through. You are less alone than you think. Talk to the medical staff at your hospital, especially the nurses and Playleader. Get in touch with a parents' organisation (see the back of this book). You will surely find a sympathetic ear to help you through these anxious times.

GUILT

This is a very difficult feeling to come to terms with. In most cases there is no clear reason why your child was born with a heart defect, but it does not stop you searching for a reason. You may find yourself asking futile questions in an attempt to rationalise it. Was it the medication I took? what about that cold virus I had? and so on. You might find some comfort from the clever people at the very centre of modern heart research. THEY don't know how it happens either.

So learn to recognise the questions that lead to a sense of guilt. If you could have prevented the heart defect, you would have done, wouldn't you?

You and your family are NOT TO BLAME.

Later you will quite often find that you have built new caring friendships with people you hardly knew. And our children, who are much more resilient than most of us imagine, often become more self-reliant as a result of these experiences.

However do remember to maintain communications with the rest of your family at least by phone. Sometimes even though things look bleak at the hospital, it is wise to go home for a few hours if practicable. It is amazing how this can put things back in perspective. It's good for parents and the rest of the family.

FATHERS

If you are the father, your way of coping with your child and with the worry of your child's condition may be different from your partner's. Most fathers must work to earn money to keep the home and family together. This means that you may not have time to take the child to clinic, or to spend time with him at hospital. So the mother usually has the responsibility of these jobs. They can be a great strain, and you can help your partner by letting her know that you realise this and try to understand.

A few fathers become so involved in their work and the need to provide, that they end up by having less time for their families than ever before. This need to work and become involved outside the home, is a way of trying to cope with a difficult situation.

You may find yourself ignoring or avoiding the situation by working too hard, drinking too much, or continually doing things that give you no time to think of your family or to help them. You could be depriving them of the support of your presence when they need it most.

One of the best ways you, as a father, can help is by making a point of visiting your child in hospital as often as you can. Visiting time for parents is very flexible and some fathers have found that evening visits, when they can stay until the child is asleep, fit in well with their working days.

It will be helpful for you, if you can visit when doctors are doing their ward rounds. There are times when they would prefer to discuss your child's condition with both parents present. This means you get information first-hand and are able to get answers to any questions you might have. It also helps you feel that you are not being left out. To have a child with a heart condition is not an everyday problem. It is a situation that is almost impossible for one person to cope with on their own. So even if you feel your partner is holding up very well, she will appreciate your presence and moral support. You may be amazed at the strength of your partner in these difficult times. You may ask yourself, 'Is she doing so well because she has no alternative?' You might ask if there is more that you could do to support your partner.

Your partner may take it for granted that you will not want to play a leading part. As a father you may feel left out and helpless. You may feel you are not needed, that things seem to go along very well without you. In fact, you are needed by everyone, especially your child and everyone concerned with the care of your child.

You may find it harder than your partner does to accept the fact that your child has a heart problem. Sometimes, with a new baby, you may feel that you do not want to become too attached to your child in case he or she dies. A heart defect is rather scary, but it has happened. The best thing you can do is to try to accept it, and do the best you can for your child.

Men have fears and worries too, and if you talk about them it will help ease the pressure. If you feel left out, admitting this to someone may be the first step towards finding a solution to the problem. Comparatively few men do share their feelings. Many seem to feel they should be able to cope alone, but few people can go it alone successfully with no outside help. It is stronger to ask for help than to pretend you don't need it.

REACTIONS OF OTHERS

It is fair to say that the majority of your friends, acquaintances, neighbours — and colleagues at work will be totally uncomprehending of the difficulties of having a 'heart' child. Generally you will find that they fall into two sorts. The first make wildly simplifed

judgements 'Oh, you needn't worry, heart problems they're easily fixed these days' . . . The other group over-react in totally the opposite direction 'However will you cope? — my brother's neighbour's little girl is really bad with that'.

The latter group are often worse than useless and cross the road when they see you coming to avoid being upset by your 'news'.

And you will meet still more who will alarm you by blurting out astonishingly tactless comments.

Comfort yourself by remembering that you understand the reality of the situation in a way that 90% of these people never will. Also that there are many who just can't handle your problem and simply don't know what to say to you. They react by avoiding you. It is not you they are rejecting — it is your situation.

On the positive side you will probably find a few key people who will step forward to become a tower of strength to you!

You will learn a lot about people when you have a heart child!

4 LIVING WITH A HEART CHILD
Coming home

Bringing your baby home from hospital is usually a time for celebration. If, however, your baby has been diagnosed as having a heart defect, or indeed has already undergone some investigation or surgery, the celebration will be coupled with more than the usual anxiety. Many parents worry about how they will cope with the full responsibility of caring for their baby which, up until now, has been shared with hospital staff. You may find yourself constantly checking your baby and worrying when, for example, he appears more restless, or seems to be crying more than usual. It is very easy to fall into the trap of attributing every change in your baby's behaviour to his condition, completely forgetting that 'normal' babies also go through spells of fretfulness, lack of appetite, not sleeping and so on. Some parents have found that slightly raising the head of the cot has helped their baby sleep more comfortably.

Coping alone

The first few months of living with a heart baby are never easy. Even if your baby is a relatively good feeder there is still the problem of coming to terms with his condition to cope with. Before we have a heart baby the most the majority of us know about the heart is that if it stops, that is it. We are culturally bound to the idea that the heart is the source of life, and therefore the news that there is something wrong with our baby's heart has particularly emotive connotations. Somehow we have to make the leap from knowing very little about how the heart works to understanding that babies with even very complex problems can and do survive. And we have to do this at a time when just coping with our baby's needs takes up all our time and energy. If, as in many cases, your baby is a poor feeder, tires easily, falls asleep in the middle of his feed and then wakes up screaming an hour later, and maintains this pattern at night as well, you may well feel as though you are living a waking nightmare. The important fact to hold onto during this time is that things will get better. As your baby begins to grow you will be able to increase gradually the amount of food he can take and as you get to know him better you will be more relaxed caring for him. Initially, however, it is very hard and if you have an older child or children to look after as well you will need help. Don't be afraid to ask for it from friends, relatives, your health visitor and of course your husband. If your baby is bottle-fed or you can get him to take milk from a bottle as well, let your husband give the evening feed while you have an early night. If friends come during the day with offers of help, accept it gladly, point them in the direction of the ironing board or vacuum cleaner. If you are feeling in need of a break leave them with the baby while you take your other child to the park, or go and do some shopping.

Staying sane!

Babies are remarkable barometers of their mother's emotions, so the more anxious and worried you are feeling the more quickly your baby will 'home in' and react adversely to your feelings, which in turn will obviously affect you. One can very easily get into a seemingly endless cycle of worry and tension; it does help to be aware of this and try and break the cycle before it goes too far. If you feel things starting to get on top of you, try and leave your baby or child with a trusted friend or relative, even if it is only for an hour and get out. Do anything that makes a change from your normal routine so that you have the opportunity to distance yourself from your problem, even for a short time. Anxiety is a strong emotion which creates energy: giving it an outlet, such as a long, brisk walk, gardening, or, in the absence of anything else, kicking 'hell' out of a cardboard box or similar, (nothing hard, it will hurt your feet). This does help relieve the tension, even if it doesn't do much for the cardboard box! Parents have found that giving their anxiety an outlet helps them provide a positive, emotionally stable environment for their children. Trying to protect those around you, including your other children and your heart child as he grows older, by keeping your worries to yourself does not usually benefit anyone. Children easily pick up your anxiety and because you do not talk about it they in turn become worried that it is 'too bad' to talk about.

BACK TO NORMALITY
The separation and splitting up of the family while your child is in hospital is one of the things that may cause problems when surgery is hopefully behind you and you come home expecting to be on top of the world and everything to be wonderful. You may not — and it may not be! Many parents talk of returning home and feeling very depressed. If their child has done well they feel guilty about this and cannot understand why they feel so low.

But really it is not easy taking back sole responsibility for your child's care, particularly if he may not yet be doing as well as you hoped, when before there was always medical advice and support on tap. Also, for many weeks prior to and during hospitalisation you have been living on nervous energy, all other considerations not to do with your child become irrelevant. It takes quite an adjustment to get back into the routine of work, cooking, shopping, etc, which sometimes seem very mundane in comparison.

Coping with a convalescent child who clings to you and is faddy about food, is not easy. Add your other children who may be feeling equally insecure as a result of the separation – and you have a lot to cope with! It is important that you can accept this. Don't ask too much of yourself and *do* ask for help and advice if you are worried about anything.

GET HELP!
Let your GP know that you are home from hospital; ask for the Health Visitor to call. There is increasing liaison between Cardiac Units and the local Community Health Visitor so she should know you're home fairly soon

anyway but don't wait for her to get in touch. If you feel concerned that something really is not right with your child, phone the ward of the hospital from where you have been discharged and ask their advice. Staff are aware of how difficult the first few days at home are and will want to help if you are really worried.

Knowing that there is help available to you will help lessen that awful feeling of isolation that many parents feel once they leave hospital and begin the journey home.

When to call the doctor

One of the major worries that parents have during the early months of caring for a heart baby is knowing whether or not he is unwell. As with a normal child one of the best indicators is if he goes off his food. A sudden change in behaviour pattern, eg an unusual degree of lethargy or if the baby appears unusually pale or sweaty can also be something to watch. Usually if a baby is taking his food normally, there is no cause for concern. Most GPs are very helpful and understand your anxieties, but readily admit that they generally have very few heart children to deal with and so do not always have the information you may be looking for. Many parents find the realisation that their GP is not 'the expert' rather frightening. Who can they turn to? It may be helpful to remember that although not a specialist on children's hearts, the GP is your family doctor, knows a great deal about children's problems, the difference between being 'ill' and 'well' — and does have responsibility for your child. You should not feel you have to carry the burden alone of deciding when your child is ill. If, for example, you feel your baby is ill, it will help if you can give a clear picture to your GP as to why you feel this. If you are requesting a visit at 2am in the morning (isn't that always the time babies and children go from being 'unwell' to 'ill'?), instead of demanding that the doctor visit, take a deep breath, explain your concern and ask for advice. This puts the onus on the doctor. If your GP does not come out and, having followed advice and instruction, you are still not happy, phone again. If you voice your concern, most doctors will come out, but it is helpful for you if you can explain enough for them to make the choice. Then, next time when you need to call you will feel more confident in doing so.

VISITING OUTPATIENTS
Out-patients appointments also allow you to voice any concern you are feeling at your child's condition. Since these may occur only infrequently it is as well to go prepared. If you have several questions to ask, (and who hasn't?) write them down. Many parents complain of suffering a mental block when they are faced with a busy Out-patient Department and a doctor that they may not have seen before. Writing down in advance any questions you want to ask, helps overcome this problem.

Growing up

ACTIVITY, DISCIPLINE

If bringing up a healthy child is difficult enough, bringing up a child who has a heart condition inevitably presents us with problems we've not even thought of before, let alone had to deal with. We are continually beset with questions; To what extent should I enforce discipline? How much exertion can I allow? What about school, will he cope in a normal school environment? It sometimes helps to turn the whole situation around and try to change the emphasis. Not 'here is a heart child, what can he do?', but 'here is an ordinary child who happens to have a heart condition, is there anything he cannot do?'. Young children with heart conditions usually know their own physical limits, more so than adults, and almost never overtax themselves, therefore it is unnecessary to restrict their activities. Older children with major heart problems may have to avoid over-strenuous exertion and will start to become aware that they cannot always keep up with their playmates at school. Depending on your child's personality, this can cause a great deal of frustration and it may be wise to start thinking of some less physically demanding interest in which to involve him. Preferably something at which he can be reasonably good as his ego tends to take a hammering in other areas. For the more physically able child, indoor basketball which uses a smaller area and is played indoors may be an alternative to football or netball when the weather is cold. Drama may serve as a useful outlet for some children. Giving your child a pet of his own to take care of is another possibility. The main thing to strive for, is as full and normal a life as possible and to try and avoid imposing unnecessary restraints.

No restrictions need to be put on children with minor defects.

Discipline is basically a matter of teaching a child the rules by which he can live as an acceptable member of society. Therefore, we are doing any child a disservice if we do not teach him these rules. Many parents complain that their 'heart' children are unusually irritable, tearful and lacking in concentration. Clearly some children do have a lower tolerance level, particularly prior to corrective surgery. Somehow, as parents, we have to try and walk a tightrope between accepting that there are times when our children find just 'carrying on as normal' more than they can cope with and teaching them that rudeness, temper tantrums, etc are not acceptable modes of behaviour.

SCHOOLING

The problems your child encounters at school will clearly depend on the severity and nature of his heart problem. Most parents find that schools welcome their child and do their best to provide for any extra needs that the child may have. If it is not advisable for him to go out in very cold weather, some schools may have overcome the problem by giving him a job to do indoors, eg looking after any class-room pets, watering the plants etc. Or he may be able to choose a friend to keep him company in the class-room or school hall during play-time. Some children with more severe defects may be eligible for a welfare helper who comes into the school specifically to help that child. This may in itself cause problems, as all children hate being different. The degree of exposure the helper has will depend on circumstances: often it is possible for a helper to blend into the background and not be too obviously caring for one child. The amount of help available does vary among Education Authorities and having a concerned, caring head-teacher will help considerably. It is usually advisable to make an appointment to see the head-teacher well before your child is due to start school and find out how flexible he is prepared to be in overcoming any problems.

HELPING SIBLINGS COPE

It is sometimes difficult for other children in your family to understand why their brother or sister may be the object of extra attention from grandparents and other relatives or friends. It is natural they may feel some resentment about this and they will find it easier to cope if they are helped to understand why it occurs. This may be particularly the case when your 'heart baby' is first born. An older brother or sister, if their baby brother or sister's illness is not explained, may feel that they are responsible for the illness because of naturally occurring jealousy at the new arrival. An older child of pre-school age may not understand any more than that the baby is ill, but they can be encouraged to help with simple fetching and carrying tasks and be included in bathing and changing rituals, this will

help children feel included and less anxious about the strain their parents are clearly under. When the baby is older, brothers and sisters need to be kept in touch with the situation. If hospitalisation is necessary, they will be better able to cope with the separation from both their parents and sibling if it has been talked over with them so they know why it has to occur and exactly who will be looking after them while mum and/or dad is away at the hospital.

Outside support

Some people who have never had a sick child find it very difficult to understand what a strain it can be. It is very difficult to explain the sense of isolation one can feel when faced with the never-ending questions entailed in bringing up a heart baby. Why isn't he putting on weight? What will they say at the next hospital appointment? Is it normal for him to be late sitting up, crawling, walking? Does he seem more breathless/bluer than usual? It seems impossible sometimes to find someone willing to listen to your anxieties for as long as you want to voice them. Friends may expect you to react in a certain way, or they may react in a way you find difficult to accept. You may mention to a friend that you are worried about some aspect of your baby's condition, to have that friend reply that her 'non heart' baby is 'just the same'. If you are looking for a sounding board at that particular time, this quite harmless reply may be reassuring or may be quite incredibly irritating. Other mothers wonder what to say to well-meaning strangers who look at their blue-tinged children and ask if they are wrapped up warmly enough: there will be times when you will feel as if no one understands your problems at all. But do not cut people out of your life because they appear to be out of sympathy with you at a particular time. The support of others will become more important to you as your child grows, try not to become so involved in him that you have no room for anyone else. Try to maintain some outside interests; many parents have found joining a support group helps to put things into perspective. If you are feeling particularly anxious about how your baby will cope as he grows up, seeing another child with an equally severe problem coping well may help ease your fears and encourage you to feel more optimistic about the future.

5 FEEDING PROBLEMS
Hints and tips

Generally, babies with heart defects should be treated like healthy babies and fed either by breast or by bottle according to your wishes. You may find though that your baby tires easily while feeding and smaller more frequent feeds may be necessary.

Breast feeding is recommended as breast milk is a complete food and has immunological benefits (ie, some of the immunities to disease that his mother has are passed on to the baby through the breast milk).

It may be that your baby is separated from you as a newborn because he needs specialist treatment. In this case you can express your milk at four hourly intervals and your milk can be deep frozen and kept for your baby to have. Do not worry if your production of milk seems to diminish during times of stress — continue to express at regular intervals and make sure you drink adequate amounts, then once the baby is able to suck again, the milk supply will increase to meet the baby's demand. (Most hospitals have electric breast pumps and your local National Childbirth Trust may well be able to lend you one for use at home. Most chemists sell hand breast-pumps).

Certain heart defects, which cause the baby to be breathless may mean that your baby is unable to feed either by breast or bottle initially. If this happens you will find that the nurse will pass a fine tube through the baby's nose down to his stomach and small amounts of milk will be given frequently.

As the baby's condition improves he may be able to take a little of his feed orally either from the breast or the bottle and have the remainder through the tube.

In order to estimate how much milk a breastfed baby has taken, he is 'test-weighed'. Before his feed he is changed and made comfortable, then weighed with all his clothes. The feed is given and he is weighed again with the same clothes and nappy. The number of grammes he has gained is roughly equivalent to the number of millilitres of milk he has drunk.

Sometimes if a baby finds sucking just too difficult, the feed may be given with a spoon. A small amount of rice-based cereal may be used to thicken the feed slightly.

Your baby may be slower to gain weight than others, but as long as he seems contented and sleeps for reasonable periods, do not worry too much about this. He may require feeding through the night for longer than other babies because he cannot take long feeds, but once he starts sleeping through do not worry about waking him (you need your sleep too!). If necessary fit in an extra feed during the day.

If you find that you just cannot cope with breast-feeding do not feel guilty about bottle-feeding. It will not harm your baby to have another milk. Some babies seem to prefer bottle-feeds and some find it easier to suck from a bottle. The important thing is that you and the baby should be as contented as possible!

WEANING YOUR BABY

Solid food may be introduced from round about four months of age (earlier if weight is a real problem). Start with Baby Rice or mashed banana. Use a small spoon. Do not be tempted to put cereal into the bottle because the baby would have to suck harder. Gradually introduce different feeds, but remember that babies do not need extra salt, sugar or other flavourings. (Initially try and avoid wheat-based cereals as there is some evidence that babies can develop malabsorption problems if given wheat too early). You will find that your baby will establish his own routines and eventually need only three or four feeds a day at normal mealtimes.

"Ugh I don't like it . . ." Feeding 'heart' babies and toddlers often requires lots of patience!

6 WHEN IT IS TIME FOR AN OPERATION

When the time comes for your child to have the operation, it is best to be as well prepared as possible so that you can in turn help your child. You may already have been in the ward. You may have thought how frightening it all looks; all that machinery, with nurses and doctors rushing round all looking very busy, children attached to strange equipment, tubes and wires everywhere and babies hardly visible amongst it all! To the uninitiated this is exactly how it seems! By this time you will have had a chance to find out what is wrong with your child's heart and what the operation involves. If you

have not been able to do so and your own doctor at home has not been able to help (in such a specialised subject, not every general practitioner may know about all the recent advances in heart surgery) do not hesitate to get in touch with the doctors at the hospital. They will be very happy to explain the situation to you, and will always discuss the forthcoming operation with you in detail. Your local Parents' Support group will also be able to help you by introducing you to a parent whose child has had heart surgery. See chapter 15 for more information.

Giving your consent

It is not unusual to have doubts about giving consent for such a big operation to be performed on your child. If he is handicapped in any way because of his heart defect, the decision to give consent will probably be easier than if to all intents and purposes your child is leading a normal and active life. However, if the doctors have explained that an operation is necessary, it is because the child's defect, if not corrected before he is much older, will cause considerable damage to his heart muscle or to his lungs. Unfortunately, there are still some defects which cannot be totally corrected. It may be that the purpose of the operation to be performed is to improve, but not to

correct and is termed a palliative one. But again, your doctors will not advise an operation unless they and their colleagues feel that it will help your child to lead an easier and happier life.

When the operation is planned, the process of consent is often spread over several weeks or months involving consultations in the out patients department. However, if the operation is urgent this process is naturally shortened. It is extremely important to ask the doctors to explain simply and carefully to you the problems and risks involved, so that you are fully in the picture.

What shall I tell my child? – getting used to the hospital

If your child is old enough to talk, then talk to him about going into hospital. The older he is, the longer he needs to get used to the idea. He will probably have been in hospital before, so remind him of the 'pleasant' things about his stay or to remember what the doctor or nurse did. Let him play out these situations with his teddy. Stick a plaster on teddy's leg or chest for example. Buy a toy stethoscope and let him listen to teddy's chest. Playmobile have sets of play people and equipment for hospital work and operating theatre. These are very useful in getting children to play about their forthcoming hospital stay. If he is old enough to understand about his heart being abnormal, then you can tell him that his heart is going to be made better so that he does not get so puffed when he runs for instance. Tell him as much about the operation as you think he can understand and answer all his questions as you are able. Do not try

Explaining what's going to happen

to change the subject in order to spare his feelings. It is far better for him to talk about his fears than to keep them bottled up. You may say that most children seem to forget all about what happens during this time and that you will be staying in the hospital near him and making sure that he is all right.

Pre-operation tests

Your child will be admitted a few days before the operation in order for various tests to be carried out and also for him to get used to his surroundings and to meet the doctors and nurses who will be looking after him following his surgery.

The day before admission, let him pack a special bag with some of his favourite toys and make sure to include any 'comforters', blankets, special feeding cups or bottles, etc.

When you arrive you will be taken to the ward, which may not necessarily be the one in which he will be nursed post-operatively. You will meet all the staff (see Who's Who on page 37).

A doctor will examine your child and go through his medical history. The pre-operative tests are important as they will give the doctors information on which to base the post-operative treatment. They will be:
1 Blood test — blood will be taken

29

from a vein in the arm in order to match up the blood to be used for the operation. If your child is blue this may be difficult as the blood tends to 'clot' very quickly and it may have to be repeated.

2 Chest X-ray
3 Electrocardiogram (ECG)
4 Echocardiogram

5 Throat swab — a sterile cotton wool bud is wiped over the back of the throat and is sent to the laboratory to ensure that there is no infection.
6 A urine specimen may also be sent to the laboratory to rule out infection (if your child is not 'potty' trained a plastic bag is stuck to the genital area to catch the urine).

The day before the operation

The day before, you will meet the surgeon who is to perform the operation. He will explain in detail with diagrams if necessary, what he plans to do and then he will ask you to sign a form saying that you consent to the operation.

You will also, on this day, be shown the Intensive Care Unit. This is where your child will return immediately after surgery. You will probably be able to see another child in this room with all the 'machinery' attached. On return from theatre, your child will be attached to a number of pieces of equipment, none of which will cause him much discomfort, although it will be difficult for him to move around.

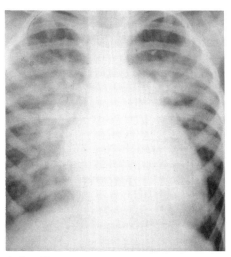

A chest X-ray

Equipment that helps recovery – what it all does – the I.T.U.

If he is to be 'ventilated', that is, if it is necessary to have his 'breathing' done for him by a ventilator (and this is quite usual after by-pass surgery and some of the other operations) he will have a tube down his nose or mouth into his windpipe. This allows for the passage of air and oxygen from the ventilator to the lungs and back from the lungs. This tube may be attached to his forehead

with a band of strapping all round his head to stop the tube being dislodged. This tube is attached to a longer length of tubing which in turn is connected to the ventilator — a small machine standing beside the bed. If your child is able to breathe completely unaided he will be nursed with an oxygen facemask or in a head-box if he is small enough. Moisture is added to the oxygen, which makes it misty in order to keep his chest secretions loose and easier for him to cough up.

He will have another tube down his nose into his stomach allowing secretions to drain out and so prevent him from being sick. He may have a 'drip' going into a vein on one side of his neck. This is so that he can be fed with fluids for at least the first 24 hours. Both arms may be splinted so that he cannot move them. There will be further tubes into veins and an artery to provide means of transfusing him with blood or other fluid, to measure his blood pressure and to give some drugs if necessary. The arterial tube is there for two purposes.

a) Arterial (red) blood can be easily obtained from this tube for sampling purposes. Frequent checks have to be made on the gas and chemical content of the blood to make sure that all the body systems are functioning correctly. This saves your child having frequent 'pricks'.

b) The blood pressure can be measured continuously. This also saves the child from being disturbed to have a blood pressure cuff put round his arm or leg each time. The pressure is shown on a television screen along with other tracings, which are constantly monitored with the help of electrodes.

The operation scar will be either down the middle of the chest or under the arm. On return to the ward he will have a dressing over the wound. There will be one or two tubes coming out of his chest to drain off any fluid left in the chest cavity or around the heart. The amount is measured and a similar quantity of blood or other fluid is replaced. In those children who have had bypass surgery, there are two 'wires' also coming out of the chest which are usually rolled up and attached to the chest in little packets and not used. They are put in routinely at the end of the operation in case the natural pacing mechanism of the heart is temporarily affected by the surgery. The heart may need artificial pacing from a battery driven pacemaker which

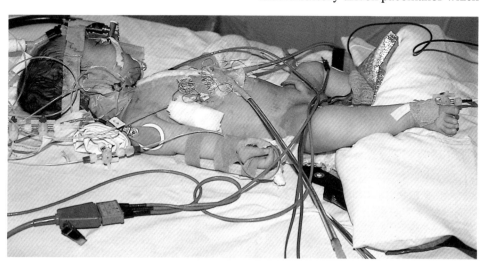

In the Intensive Care Unit

31

hangs in a small box at the end of the bed and to which the wires can easily be attached. Finally, in the post bypass patients again, there is a tube which drains the bladder of all the urine. Another machine you may see in the Intensive Care Unit is the portable X-ray machine with which chest X-rays are taken while the children are lying flat on their backs.

When you have your first visit to the Intensive Care Unit it is most unlikely and wants to see the Intensive Care Unit, he may certainly do so, but he should not be forced to see it. Just tell him that he will be in a special room, where there will be machines to help him in every way, even to breathe. He will not be able to talk, but he will hear people talking and he will be able to mouth words and the nurses will be able to understand him. Another thing he should know is that for the first day he will not be able to have anything to

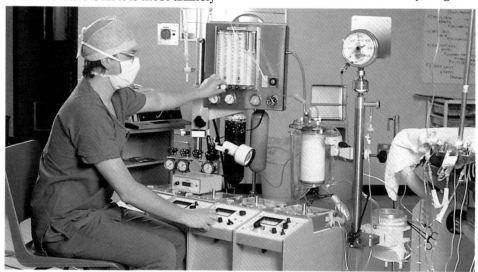

The Heart-Lung by-pass machine

that you will be able to take in all of these things, but here again, do not be afraid to ask about anything you do not understand. If your child is old enough drink. His mouth will feel very dry, but the nurses will wet his mouth to make it feel better, with some cotton wool dipped in water.

The hours before the operation

The evening before the operation your child will have a special 'bubble' bath with antiseptic solution in the water to make sure that his skin is really clean. Before he is ready for bed, he will be given a sedative to ensure that he has a good night's sleep. Four hours before the operation he will be given a glucose drink. About one hour, before he will be given his premedication, probably an injection, which will make him sleepy. Tell him that you will see him as soon as the operation is over.

32

He will go to the operating theatre with one of the ward nurses, in her arms if he is small enough or on a trolley if he is too heavy to carry.

The operation has arrived . . .

For you now, the next few hours will probably seem the longest hours of your life. If the weather is good, it is an idea for you to go out for a walk, or to go shopping, or to visit a museum, anything in fact to while away the time. You will be told an approximate time to return to the Unit. A bypass operation can take anything from 3-6 hours and the other operations take about 2-4 hours, but delays are frequent and do not mean that anything has gone wrong.

After the operation

When he is ready to return, his bed, which has been specially prepared, is taken to the theatre and he is transferred from the theatre table straight onto his bed, which is then wheeled back to the ward. In the I.T.U., he is attached to all the measuring equipment mentioned before. He will then have his chest X-rayed. After all this which takes about twenty minutes you will be taken to see him. He will probably be asleep because the children are kept well sedated for the first 24 hours. Do not be upset though if he is awake, because if you ask him later on, you will find that he will remember very little about that first day.

During this time there will be a nurse and a doctor looking after your child. You will be able to come and visit whenever you like but nobody will expect you to stay for long periods. Your child will be well sedated and probably will remember very little of this time. Most units will ask that you check with a member of staff before entering as these are busy times, with doctors and nurses often having to concentrate specially hard on your child's care. The nurse will be constantly attending your child checking on everything at least every fifteen minutes. Although the machines help the nurses and doctors a great deal, they still cannot do the actual nursing! You will notice on occasions that the nurse will encourage your child to cough by applying suction to the tube in his windpipe, the nostrils and the mouth. This is done to prevent pooling of secretions in the lungs and the onset of chest infection. Chest physiotherapy will be given regularly by the physiotherapist.

The attention goes on throughout the night. You are advised to take advantage of the beds provided for you nearby because the day will have been mentally very exhausting for you. If, for any reason, the doctors are worried or there is anything they think you should know, they will contact you. Conversely, if you wake up during the night and want to know how your child is, all you have to do is dial the internal number of the ward and you may talk to sister or staff nurse.

The next morning after various tests, including blood tests and a chest X-ray, the tubes in the chest will probably be removed. As the day progresses most of the other tubes will be removed. He will be weaned off the ventilator if that has been necessary and once he is breathing on his own then the tube will be removed from his windpipe. He will start having small drinks and later, light diet.

The rate of progress varies from child to child depending on the severity of the heart defect and the sort of operation performed. The removal of all the tubes may take up to a week or even longer, so do not be disappointed if your child seems to be taking longer than another. When he does start to drink, the amount of fluid given has to be limited for at least the first 48 hours because if he has too much , the kidneys may not be able to function properly. Therefore, you will be asked to measure all the fluid your child drinks.

Once most of the tubes have been removed your child will be transferred from the Intensive Care Unit to another room. On the third day post-operatively he may well be able to sit out of bed or even walk a little. Gradually he will return to normal activity, but you will notice that he will be tired and probably rather irritable and miserable. This is a normal reaction — commonly known as 'post-op blues'

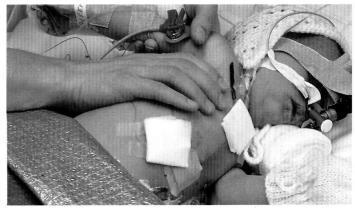

Physiotheraphy after the operation

and you should encourage your child to rest as much as possible and he will gradually revert to his normal self.

A few days later he will probably have his pacemaker wires and the couple of drain stitches removed. This does not hurt, but he will feel the skin being pulled a little. If everything has gone according to plan, your child will probably be allowed home 7-10 days after the operation, but it is not uncommon for some to have to stay three or four weeks. It is very difficult to guarantee the actual date of discharge home so it is best to just wait and see!

During the course of recovery most children will have been given several medicines and it is likely that he will have to take some when he does go home (see chapter 9).

You will be given a supply to take with you and you should continue these until your child comes back for his Out-patient appointment check-up which will be about four weeks after discharge. If you run out before then, your own doctor at home will be able to prescribe more.

Possible complications

As with all operations, there may be some complications following the surgery. These may include:

1 BLEEDING

Immediately after the operation, especially if it is not the child's first operation, there is the possibility that he will bleed excessively from his operation site. The drains in the wound have to be kept clear so that the blood may drain freely and more often than not the bleeding will stop spontaneously. If however it persists, it may be necessary for the child to return to the operating theatre for the surgeon to investigate and maybe put an extra stitch into the heart. There's always enough blood ready to give the child to replace what he has lost and it is not usually a major problem.

2 ARRHYTHMIAS

Sometimes during cardiac surgery the natural pacing mechanisms in the heart become swollen resulting in an irregular or slow heart beat. Temporary pacing with the use of an external pacemaker may be necessary and in rare instances a permanent pacemaker may be required (see page 70). Occasionally the heart beats very fast and medicines are given on a regular basis to slow it down.

3 PARALYSED DIAPHRAGM

Sometimes during complex surgery in the chest, the phrenic nerve may be damaged or become swollen. This has an effect on the movement of the right or left diaphragm, which in turn affects the breathing pattern of the child. In children under one year of age this may cause difficulties in weaning them from the ventilator and often it may be necessary to 'plicate', that is to fix the diaphragm, to stop its abnormal movement. This necessitates another small operation.

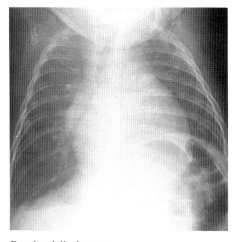

Paralysed diaphragm:
X-ray showing high left diaphragm

4 INFECTION

Infection is always a danger after any operation. Because after cardiac surgery the child is ventilated by an artificial airway, chest infections can be a problem. These can be treated with appropriate antibiotics. Should the infection get into the bloodstream (septicaemia) then a longer course of antibiotics might be required. Very rarely the wound may become infected. Again antibiotics will be given, but if the infection is deep within the wound it might be necessary for the child to return to the operating theatre and have the whole wound area cleaned and restitched.

5 RENAL FAILURE

After a long operation carried out with the heart lung bypass machine the kidneys may not be able to excrete fluid and waste matter as well as they should. Following surgery the amount of urine passed each hour is carefully measured.

If the amount passed is not sufficient then peritoneal dialysis might be introduced. This involves inserting a fine tube into the abdomen and washing out the peritoneal cavity with strong fluid which draws out the impurities in the blood.

A measured amount of fluid is inserted and then drained out each hour until the kidneys start working properly.

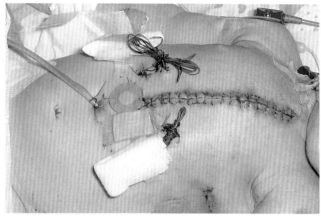

Peritoneal dialysis catheter in upper abdomen. Coiled pacing wires also shown.

6 BRAIN DAMAGE

This is the complication about which parents worry the most, but fortunately it is rare. If the child is in a poor state post-operatively with very low blood pressure then there is a possibility that the brain may not be receiving an adequate blood supply despite all the appropriate treatment. This may cause unconsciousness or convulsions. This is usually short lived and most children make a full recovery. Another reason for convulsions may be abnormal blood chemistry, such as low blood sugar or calcium levels. Blood is checked regularly for these and other levels and the situation corrected as necessary. High temperatures may cause convulsions, especially in the young child. For that reason you will notice that if the child's temperature is increasing, then every effort is made to cool him down. If the child has suffered from any of these complications, a check electroencephalogram — a test on brain waves — and often a brain scan are performed to see if there has been any damage to the brain.

In the instance where there is evidence of damage, usually it is of short duration with good recovery. Sadly in very rare instances, there may be lasting problems.

Please note that by telling you about these complications we are not saying that they *will* happen, merely that they *might* be a possibility.

7 WHO'S WHO IN HOSPITAL

PEDIATRIC CARDIOLOGIST — this is the doctor who will find out exactly what is wrong with your child's heart. He will be in charge of your child's care while he is in hospital and also in outpatients. He will arrange the cardiac catheterisation and echocardiogram

PEDIATRIC CARDIAC SURGEON — (known as 'Mr' rather than 'Dr'). This is the doctor who will perform the operation on your child's heart. He will talk to you before and after the operation explaining it all. Each of these doctors has a team to help him. They are Registrars and House Officers who will all be involved in the care of your child, performing the investigations, and helping with the operations.

INTENSIVIST — this is the doctor who will look after your child while he is in the intensive care unit immediately after the operation.

ANAESTHETIST — this is the doctor who will administer the anaesthetic to your child so that he is asleep and free from pain during and immediately following the operation. He will also look after the ventilation of your baby at any stage should he need help with his breathing.

WARD SISTER — (Charge Nurse if a man) — is in charge of the ward and of all the nurses working in it.

STAFF NURSE — a trained nurse who will look after your child while he is in hospital.

ENROLLED NURSE (EN) — also a trained nurse (but with a different sort of training) who will look after your child.

STUDENT NURSE — he/she is there to learn and to gain experience and is supervised by the staff nurses and sisters.

PLAYLEADER — she is there to help entertain your child and through play help him to understand what the doctors and nurses are doing. She will help prepare him for his operation.

WARD RECEPTIONIST — this is the person who often answers the telephone, helps the doctors and nurses with a great deal of the paperwork necessary on the ward.

PHYSIOTHERAPIST — this lady (or man) will encourage your child to expand his lungs and breathe properly after his operation. She will also help him to get out of bed and move normally.

RADIOGRAPHER — this is the person who will take X-ray pictures of your child's chest either in the X-ray department or with a portable machine in the ward.

ECG TECHNICIAN — this person will make an electrocardiographic recording of your child's heart beat.

LABORATORY TECHNICIAN — this person may come to take blood specimens from your child for special tests.

PHARMACIST — he/she will make up all the medicine that your child needs.

CHAPLAIN — you will find that there are representatives of all the main religious denominations visiting the hospital. If you wish to see one of them, just ask your ward sister and she will arrange it.

SOCIAL WORKER — if you have any problems, social or financial concerning your child or the rest of the family, a social worker will be available to discuss these with you and to help as far as she can.

THEATRE SISTER OR STAFF NURSES — these nurses assist the surgeons while they operate on your baby.

PERFUSIONIST — a technician who looks after the heart/lung bypass machine used during operations.

INTENSIVIST

ANAESTHETIST

SURGEON

RADIOGRAPHER

THEATRE SISTER

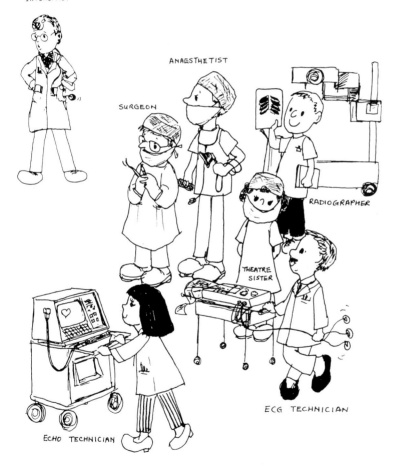

ECHO TECHNICIAN

ECG TECHNICIAN

8 SOME GENERAL ADVICE
Answers to questions most parents ask

1 Causes of Congenital Heart Disease

The heart forms during the first ten weeks of pregnancy and it is during this time that abnormalities occur. The cause in over 90% of cases is unknown. It appears to be a mixture of our complex genetic make-up and some trigger from the environment. It is important to say that it is NO-ONE'S fault. Some factors, however, are known. For example when the heart is involved in general chromosomal abnormalities such as Down's syndrome or a gene problem such as Marfan's syndrome. Occasionally the heart is damaged by an infection such as German measles, or by drugs or medications such as excess alcohol or some anticonvulsants.

2 Immunizations

Whooping cough can be a very serious illness in children with heart problems, and unless there is a definite contra-indication, the child should be protected. All other immunizations, diptheria, tetanus, polio, mumps, measles and rubella should be given routinely. The new measles, mumps and rubella vaccine should be given and it is expected that all three infections will become much less common. BCG is also important if indicated.

3 Infections

Infections should be treated as in the normal child. Blue children when they have a high temperature require lots to drink to prevent dehydration which may further thicken their already abnormally thick blood. If vomiting is a significant problem then it is important to call your doctor.

4 Schooling

The vast majority of children are able to attend normal schools, and can join in all normal activities. Children, who remain significantly blue, tolerate cold weather poorly, and perhaps special arrangements can be made to avoid school playgrounds in inclement weather. Those who are significantly breathless should be allowed to rest when they become tired. The children usually set their own limits far better than anyone else. In senior school, there are a few conditions in which competitive sport, judo, rowing and karate should be avoided. These are significant aortic stenosis, pulmonary hypertension and hypertrophic cardiomyopathy. Reasonable exercise and swimming, however, should be encouraged.

5 Dental Care

It is known that patients who have bad dental hygiene with lots of caries and unhealthy gums force bacteria into their blood stream with chewing and biting. We strongly recommend regular dental visits and the use of the fluoride toothpaste and perhaps in addition, fluoride drops if there is no fluoride in the local water. The amount of fluoride in your local tapwater can be ascertained by writing or telephoning the local Community Health Service Office. Should dental treatment be required in the form of extractions, scaling, polishing and deep fillings, then the child should receive a large dose of antibiotic an hour before the dental work. This is because these procedures are known to produce bacteria in the blood stream. Many children with heart disease will need this prophylactic antibiotic therapy for the rest of their lives.

Small children with heart problems often require many medications that contain large amounts of sugar to make them palatable. Prevention of dental caries and bad gums is more difficult in our group of children.
Some useful tips are:
a) Avoid sugary foods and drinks between meals or last thing at night.
b) Teeth should be cleaned after medicines, and particularly so after the night time dose. Ask your doctor if tablets can be used rather than medicines. Ask if sugar free medicines are available.
c) Start with toothbrushes early.
d) Use fluoride toothpaste, think about added fluoride drops.
e) Plan to start visits to the dentist from about three years of age.

6 Travelling and Holidays

The majority of patients have no difficulties with air or sea flights. Do ensure that adequate medications are taken abroad. Avoid too much exposure to sun and ensure adequate hydration, particularly in small children and those who are blue. If the child is very blue or breathless, discuss your plans with your doctors. They may well advise you to inform your travel agent and the airline, and arrangements can be made for wheel-chairs and oxygen to be available for the flight. It is important to remember that although the cabins are pressurized on all flights, this is equivalent to a height of 5000 feet (1600 M). This is equivalent to breathing at the top of Ben Nevis. Most children will cope very well with this. Please allow enough time for these arrangements to be made if necessary.

7 Insurance

Life insurance may be difficult and an excess premium may be demanded. There may be some difficulty in getting insurance cover for mortgages.

There is usually no difficulty with travel insurance, but you may require a letter from your doctor saying that your child is stable and no particular complication is expected. Personal and property insurance cause no problems.

8 Smoking

Smoking produces damage to the normally smooth lining of the arteries. Clots form on this now roughened area. It is the blockage of arteries as a result of these clots that produce heart attacks and strokes. In addition, smoking produces chronic chest infections and cancer of the lung, gullet and mouth. There is no reason at all to suppose that patients with congenital heart problems will be less likely to develop these complications of smoking than the average person.

Children are much more likely to smoke if their parents smoke.

Passive smoking, that is regular breathing in other peoples exhaled smoke, causes similar problems to smoking itself.

SMOKING IS BAD FOR US ALL. SMOKING IS THE BIGGEST AVOIDABLE HEALTH HAZARD IN DEVELOPED COUNTRIES.

9 Alcohol

Small amounts cause no problem in adults. Excess is bad, causes emotional and behavioural problems and is linked to many accidents in adults and adolescents.

EXCESS ALCOHOL IS THE SECOND
LARGEST AVOIDABLE HEALTH
HAZARD IN DEVELOPED COUNTRIES.

10 Diet

A good balanced diet is important.
Babies and small children require fat to
grow at a normal rate, and also to
supply essential vitamins. In older
children and adolescents, it is
important to avoid too much fat,
particularly animal saturated fats. It is
important to avoid too much salt and
sugar, and we know that many of the
convenience foods contain lots of salt,
sugar, animal fat.

Try to use wholemeal bread,
wholewheat cereals, vegetables, fruit,
fish, relatively lean meat and
polyunsaturated fats. Try not to add
excess salt at the table. Salt in
cooking, however, is fine.

Further practical advice on diet can be
found in 3 useful booklets published by
the Health Education Authority, entitled
'Guide to Healthy Eating', 'Excercise.
Why bother?' and 'Do You Take
Sugar?'. See chapter 14 for details.

11 Weight

Obesity (excess weight) in the
adolescent and adult causes more work
for the heart to do. The fatter you are,
the more likely you are to have a high
blood pressure, and this again
increases the work of the heart and
causes damage to the artery walls.
Avoid being too thin as this is bad for
you also. Aim for the average weight
for your age and height.

12 Driving

Usually there are no problems unless
there is a risk of sudden collapse,
which is very rare. Patients who have
pacemakers inserted can hold a regular
driving licence, but are unable to hold a
heavy goods vehicle licence.

13 Contraception

Usually, normal contraceptive
practices involving the low dose
combined pill can be used in the
majority of post-operative patients,
and those with minor problems whose
hearts are functionally good, for
example – small holes, mild to
moderate valve problems. The
exceptions, however, are those
patients who have:
1 Thick blood (called polycythaemia)
2 High blood pressure in either the
lung or the body artery
3 Those with sluggish circulations,
either from weak heart muscle or from
the Fontan type operation connecting
the right atrium directly into the lung
artery
4 Those on anti-coagulants

In these cases the Progesterone only
pill, injectable Depo-Provera, or
barrier/sheath methods are suggested.
Intra-uterine coils are usually not
suitable for young women but if used
need antibiotic prophylaxis for
insertion and sometimes for removal.

PLEASE GET ADVICE EARLY FROM
YOUR LOCAL FAMILY PLANNING
ASSOCIATION.

14 Pregnancy and Delivery

If there is little in the way of
symptoms, then pregnancy is very
well tolerated. If the patient is
breathless regular supervision will be
required, often requiring extra periods
of rest particularly towards the end of
pregnancy. The delivery almost
certainly will need to be in hospital. If
blueness is a problem, there is a higher
incidence of miscarriage. Pregnancy is
felt to be unwise in those patients who
have a very high blood pressure in the
lung artery.

For more general information about
pregnancy see the very clearly written

'Pregnancy Book' from the Health Education Authority. See chapter 14 for details.

15 Future Children
The chance that any child would be born with a heart problem is approximately 1%. If there is already one child in the family with such a problem, then the risks that a further heart problem will occur in that family rise to approximately 3%. This means that the chance of a normal child from the point of view of the heart is 97%. If there are two children affected, the chances of further heart problems rise to 10%, if three children are affected in the family the risks rise to approximately 25%. Generally, the type of defect running within one family is similar.

16 Antenatal Diagnosis
Antenatal diagnosis is possible by the use of special ultrasonic equipment and skills. With these techniques it is possible to look at the developing baby's heart at about 16-18 weeks into the pregnancy, and very frequently to be able to obtain good images of the heart structure at that stage. It is offered to those families who are at somewhat higher risk than the average family, for example those with previous children with significant heart problems or diabetic mothers.

The decision as to whether the family wish to know about the new baby's heart rests with them. Obviously a normal result is very reassuring. An abnormal result brings to light many difficult problems. Careful discussions between the general practitioner, obstetrician, general paediatrician, cardiologist and most importantly of all, the family, will need to be undertaken. The advice that is offered will naturally depend on the severity of the problem that is detected. Some will be mild and decisions will, therefore, be easy. Others will be more serious and difficult decisions may need to be taken about continuing with the pregnancy.

More recently heart abnormalities may be picked up at the routine ultrasound scans undertaken to look at the whole baby. If an abnormality is detected, further detailed scans and tests would be arranged and here again careful discussion between everyone would need to take place.

17 Risks to Offspring
Accurate figures for many conditions are currently unknown, but it is likely that the children of patients who themselves have congenital heart problems will have an approximately 6-10% chance of having a heart problem. It appears that the risks to offspring are slightly higher if the mother rather than the father has the heart problem.

There is no increased risk to the children of normal brothers and sisters in a family where one child has heart disease.

18 Occupation
The majority of patients can undertake all jobs. The three services are currently very reluctant to take anyone with a heart problem, even if minor or if successfully corrected. Heavy manual work, however, may not be ideal if there is longstanding reduction in cardiac efficiency. Encouragement should be given for each child to attain his best goal academically and to take the appropriate examinations. This helps in the employment market to counterbalance the 'heart problem'.

9 MEDICINES – Drugs used to treat heart problems and what they do

Many children will not require medicines at all. Medicines are often known by two names, the chemical or generic name which is the official one, and the proprietary or company names, of which there may be several. Some children will require some of the medicines talked about below:

1 DIGOXIN

This increases the force of contraction of the heart muscle and in addition slows down conduction within the electrical system. It is used when the heart muscle needs extra support, and also in the treatment of fast heart rates.

Nausea and reduced appetite may occur as side-effects if the patient is rather sensitive to it.

2 FRUSEMIDE AND CHLOROTHIAZIDE

These are diuretics which make the kidneys pass more urine. The children lose sodium, chloride, potassium and water. When the heart is not working very well, water and salt accumulate in the body, liver and the lungs, making particularly the lungs rather heavy. When these drugs are given, the lungs become somewhat lighter, easier to expand and, less energy is used in breathing. Try to avoid excess salt when taking these drugs as this reduces their efficiency.

3 SPIRONOLACTONE/ AMILORIDE

These are weaker diuretics which hold on to potassium. They are often used in conjunction with the other diuretics.

4 POTASSIUM SUPPLEMENTS

These are used in association with diuretics when the dose of diuretics is modest. They are, unfortunately, rather unpalatable. Natural replacements in the form of orange juice, tomato juice and bananas may be used instead.

5 HYDRALAZINE AND CAPTOPRIL

These drugs dilate blood vessels and as a result reduce blood pressure. They can be used in patients with high blood pressure to reduce it to normal. They can also be used in those patients with a normal blood pressure and a weak heart. By reducing the blood pressure this reduces the work of the heart.

6 PROPRANOLOL

This reduces the rate and force of contraction of the heart muscle. It is useful in treating fast heart rates, high blood pressure and also relieving spasm of heart muscle in tetralogy of Fallot.

7 ANTIARRHYTHMIC DRUGS

Drugs that are used to control arrhythmias eg Verapamil, Disopyramide, Lignocaine, Phenytoin, Mexilitene, Flecanide and Amiodarone.

8 ANTICOAGULANTS

Children who have artificial valves made of metal and plastic require blood thinning medicines in the form of Warfarin to prevent clots developing on the valve. Regular blood tests are required to assess the level of thinning of the blood. He will be given a card on which are recorded the Warfarin dosage and the result of the blood test. Aspirin and Dipyridamole are sometimes used to prevent the blood platelets sticking together post-operatively. Anticoagulants are often used in adolescent patients with large weak hearts, and also those with high blood pressure in the lung arteries.

9 SEDATIVES

Children with heart problems are sometimes very fractious and mild sedation, for example Trichloryl is often very helpful in allaying anxiety and ensuring adequate rest for the child.

10 ANTIBIOTICS

These are used to fight infection in the same way as for a child with a normal heart and especially to prevent endocarditis during interventional procedures.

11 INTRAVENOUS DRUGS

Very strong medications can be given directly intravenously to improve the circulation to the body and to the lungs. Examples of these are Dopamine, Adrenaline, Nitroprusside, Prostaglandin, Prostacyclin and Tolazoline.

12 PARACETAMOL)

Generally speaking, it is safe to give your child paracetamol if he has a temperature. Give the dose recommended for his age on the box.

TAKING MEDICINES

When you are given a new medicine please check the following;
a) Its name
b) The reason for taking it
c) How often during the day it should be taken and its relation to meals.
d) For how long
e) Does it upset any other medicines
f) What if any are the side effects that might be expected.

GIVING MEDICINES TO YOUR BABY

This can be a difficult task but obviously it is important that the baby receives the right amount of drug at the right time.

Make sure that you understand the instructions on the bottle. Give the medicine before the feed. Use a spoon, a small syringe or medicine glass (an egg-cup would do). Hold the baby firmly with his head slightly back and give not more than a third of a teaspoonful in his mouth at once. You will find that the baby will gradually get used to the strange taste of the medicine. Do not be tempted to put medicines into your baby's bottle. This would make the milk taste strange and may have the effect of putting the baby off his feeds. If your baby is sick immediately after the medicine is given, wait a while and then repeat it. Do not repeat it if there is an interval of 15-20 minutes because some drugs are absorbed quite quickly from the stomach. If vomiting is a frequent occurrence, consult your doctor.

Antibiotics are usually made up in a syrupy substance so if your older child has to have these, give him a drink of water following them so that the syrup is cleaned off his teeth.

10 SPECIFIC HEART PROBLEMS
Introduction

There are many types of heart abnormalities and the more common ones are described in this chapter. Some children have more than one problem with their heart and perhaps more than one diagram will then be relevant to that child. Do not worry if your child's condition is not specifically described here, your doctors will describe the problem very clearly to you, perhaps using the blank diagrams at the back of the book.

INNOCENT MURMURS

These normal noises are extremely common in children. Up to 25% of healthy children have these soft murmurs at different times.

The murmurs arise from the blood flow through the large veins as they return to the chest or from the blood flow around the bends of the heart. The heart in children is compact, the normal bends are quite tight and the heart rate is faster than in adults. As a result the normal flow produces a soft noise or a murmur. An analogy is the noise that water makes in a stream as it curves round a bend.

These noises are often heard at one of the routine examinations or when there is an incidental infection. They are louder when the heart is beating faster than usual eg with a temperature or if the child is particularly worried. They are usually soft, heard in one area, change with sitting or lying, frequently have a buzzing quality and are the only finding. The rest of the examination is normal.

The noise is often so typical that no tests are necessary. Any that are done are entirely normal.

The family may be reassured that all is well and the child may be discharged with a normal heart and no restrictions.

VENTRICULAR SEPTAL DEFECT (VSD)

This is a hole between the two pumping chambers (ventricles). It allows some oxygenated blood to pass from the left side back into the right side and through the lungs. The amount of the abnormal blood flow depends on the size and site of the hole as well as the pressure difference between the two sides of the heart. The abnormal flow produces the murmurs that are heard, and also the thrill that can be sometimes felt.

If the hole is small, the child is well and there are no problems. If the hole is moderate, the extra blood in the lungs makes them heavy and the baby may breathe quickly, be slow to feed with poor weight gain, and have increased chest infections. These complaints are more marked if the hole is large. The children with modest and large holes require medications, those with small ones do not.

Most will close spontaneously or get significantly smaller. Some will not and will require operation. The usual indications for operations are:
(i) Failure to progress adequately despite medication in the first year of life.

(ii) The worry about high blood pressure in the lung arteries.

(iii) The persistence of a large blood flow into the lungs at more than seven years of age.

(iv) The development of a leaking aortic valve related to the hole.

(v) Development of extra muscle in the right ventricle secondary to the abnormal blood flow.

The operation to close the hole, usually with a patch, is performed using cardiopulmonary bypass. Occasionally in small babies, or in those where there are additional significant problems, the blood flow to the lungs may be reduced by a preliminary operation — a banding, that narrows the lung artery.

Antibiotic prophylaxis is required probably for one year after the spontaneous close of the hole. If the hole is closed by an operation, then most units advise the continuance of antibiotic prophylaxis for life.

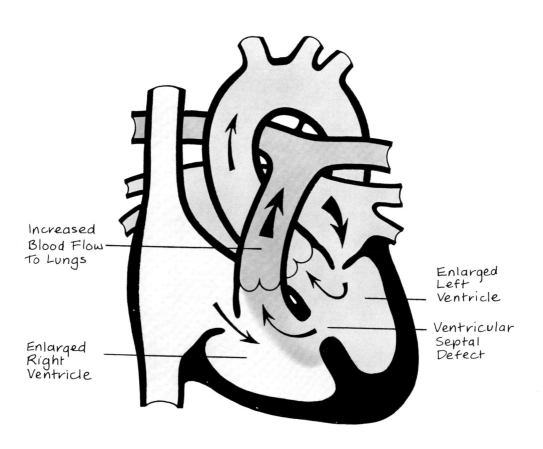

Increased Blood Flow To Lungs

Enlarged Left Ventricle

Ventricular Septal Defect

Enlarged Right Ventricle

VENTRICULAR SEPTAL DEFECT

ATRIAL SEPTAL DEFECT (ASD)

This is a hole between the two receiving chambers which allows blood from the left side to pass back to the right side and into the lungs. There are three types, the commonest is in the middle of the atrial septum (the secundum defect), sometimes it is in the lower part of the septum (the primum defect) and is associated with an abnormality (often a leak) of the mitral valve. Occasionally, it is in the top of the septum (the sinus venosus defect) associated with an abnormality of the right upper lung vein.

Usually children have no symptoms, and a routine examination finds a murmur present. Occasionally there is poor weight gain and failure to thrive. If the mitral valve is very leaky, then this may cause early symptoms of breathlessness.

Small defects that allow little blood to shunt from one side of the heart to the other often cause no problems. Such defects in the middle portion of the septum may close spontaneously in young children. Moderate and large defects do not close, and the extra work on the heart over many years into adult life causes a strain on the right side with enlargement of the receiving chamber and pump chamber. As a result the heart gets tired in middle life and the results of repairing the defect at that age are not good. The plan, therefore, is usually to have an elective repair using open heart surgery in childhood. The defect is closed either directly with a suture or patched. If it is the former, and there are no other problems, then antibiotic prophylaxis is no longer required.

If the mitral value is involved this is usually repaired with sutures at the same time as the hole is closed and antibiotic prophylaxis is required for life.

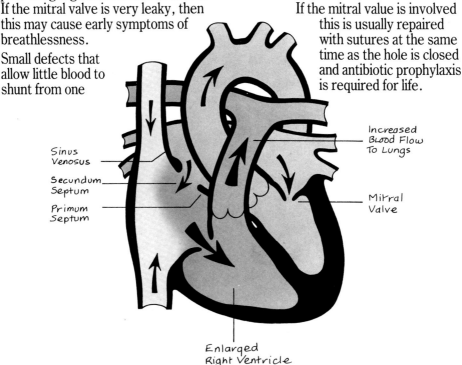

Sinus Venosus

Secundum Septum

Primum Septum

Increased Blood Flow To Lungs

Mitral Valve

Enlarged Right Ventricle

SECUNDUM ATRIAL SEPTAL DEFECT

PERSISTENT DUCTUS ARTERIOSUS (PDA)

This is a persistence of the normal tube between the aorta and the lung artery. It allows blood to pass from the high pressure aorta into the low pressure pulmonary artery and therefore increases the blood flow to the lungs. If small there are no problems, if large the child will be breathless with tiredness and poor weight gain.

It is common in premature babies.

If present for more than three months, it is unlikely to close on its own. Operation is advised to close large ones to reduce the workload on the heart and the lungs — and in small ones to prevent the chance of infection developing in this tube. The operation is performed through the left side of the chest without needing the heart/ lung machine, and the tube is tied, clipped or divided.

The circulation then returns to normal, and the child can usually be discharged from follow-up with a normal heart, and antibiotic prophylaxis is no longer required.

Closure of the ductus by catheter techniques has been performed recently. This exciting technique needs to be compared with a very excellent and safe record from surgery.

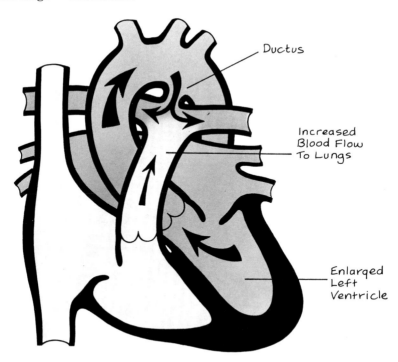

Ductus

Increased Blood Flow To Lungs

Enlarged Left Ventricle

PERSISTENT DUCTUS ARTERIOSUS

COARCTATION OF THE AORTA

This is a narrowing in the main artery to the body usually just below the origin of the left arm artery. It may be associated with abnormalities of the aortic and mitral valves. The narrowing increases the work on the left ventricle, raises the pressure in the top half of the body, and reduces it in the lower half. If severe, it can present early in life with breathlessness, difficulty to feed and occasionally very rapid deterioration in the baby's health. More moderate obstruction produces a murmur, high blood pressure, and weak pulses in the legs. With mild obstruction, a soft murmur is often picked up at school, and examination reveals weak pulses in the legs.

If the child has symptoms or high blood pressure, operation to relieve the obstruction is necessary at that stage. If the obstruction is very mild,

regular review in Out-patients is necessary. The operation is carried out through the left chest, without using the heart/lung machine. The narrow area can be directly removed, occasionally it is patched with artificial material or in small babies the first part of the left arm artery is used to effect the repair.

Long term follow-up is necessary to check on blood pressure and for any evidence of re-narrowing. This re-narrowing is more likely to occur if the operation is performed during the first three months of life. If significant re-narrowing does occur, re-operation may be necessary, or more recently stretching of this area with a balloon catheter has been successfully performed.

Some centres have recently been stretching the initial coarctation with balloon catheters in older children — with encouraging results.

Antibiotic prophylaxis is required long term.

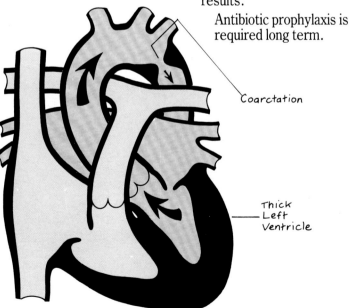

Coarctation

Thick Left Ventricle

COARCTATION OF AORTA

50

AORTIC STENOSIS

This is a narrowing between the left ventricle and the aorta. The commonest is valvar stenosis where the leaflets which are normally thin become thick and have restricted opening. This increases the work of the left ventricle. Severity is variable, and even very significant obstruction can cause no symptoms. Complaints of fainting, near fainting and breathlessness may occur and need assessment. Moderate and severe obstruction require avoidance of competitive sport, rowing, judo and karate.

Operation is required for severe obstruction and is 'open heart' surgery using the heart/lung machine. The valve would be inspected and stretched. Very occasionally it would need to be replaced at the first operation. The stretching improves the valve, but it is likely to scar up again over many years requiring further operation. Therefore long term follow-up is necessary. More recently, some centres have been stretching this valve using balloon catheters and the early results are encouraging.

With subvalvar aortic stenosis a shelf occurs between the left ventricle and the aortic valve. This requires 'open heart' surgery to remove it when the obstruction is severe. With supravalvar stenosis there is a waist above the aortic valve and above the coronary arteries. If the obstruction is severe, then this area needs to be patched again using open heart surgery.

Antibiotic prophylaxis is required life-long in all these children.

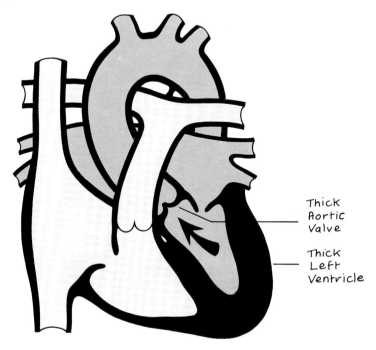

Thick Aortic Valve

Thick Left Ventricle

AORTIC VALVE STENOSIS

PULMONARY STENOSIS

The pulmonary valve leaflets are thickened and have restricted opening. The right ventricle has extra work to do and becomes thicker. If the valve is very tight, blueness will present early in life. If the obstruction is moderate, a murmur will be picked up at routine examination. Mild obstruction is tolerated very well over a long period of time. Moderate and severe obstruction require relief. The valve can be stretched and recently this has been performed more commonly by a balloon catheter rather than an operation. The short and medium term results of ballooning these valves have been very good. In some cases this is not possible, and is particularly so in small babies where the obstruction is very severe and in some older children whose valves are very thick. This may be associated with Noonan's syndrome. In these cases, an operation to stretch or remove the valve, either using open heart or closed surgery would be required.

The long term outlook is good. Mild obstructions tend not to progress after early childhood. Antibiotic prophylaxis is necessary life-long.

TETRALOGY OF FALLOT

This is a combination of a hole between the two ventricles, and a narrowing between the right ventricle and the lung artery. The right ventricle has extra work to do to squeeze blood through the narrowing to the lungs, and as it works at high pressure, is

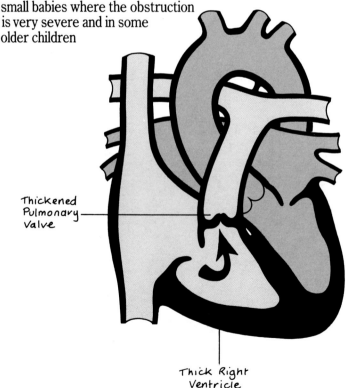

Thickened Pulmonary Valve

Thick Right Ventricle

PULMONARY VALVE STENOSIS

able to pump blood directly from it through the hole into the aorta.

A murmur may be noted initially and then blueness, breathlessness and perhaps squatting will occur during the second year. If the problem is more severe, then blueness will present earlier. Some children have 'spells' in which the blood flow to the lungs is reduced for a while. The child may cry abnormally as though in discomfort, breathe quickly, become bluer than usual and perhaps have glazed eyes, whimper and become rather limp, pale and then pass off to sleep. If these episodes occur, picking the child up and cuddling and reassuring is very helpful. Put the child over your shoulder bringing his knees up onto his tummy, so that they are between his tummy and your chest. This improves the circulation and the episode will subside. It is important to let the medical team involved know that these episodes have started to occur. Propranolol can help reduce these episodes. All children will require operation in due course. In some 'open heart' surgical repair to patch the hole and relieve the narrowing can be undertaken directly. In others, particularly if the child is small or the lung arteries are small, then a shunt operation to take extra blood into the lung arteries from an arm artery may be required. This is an operation performed through the side of the chest, and the formal repair would need to be done later. The long term results are very good. Antibiotic prophylaxis is required for life.

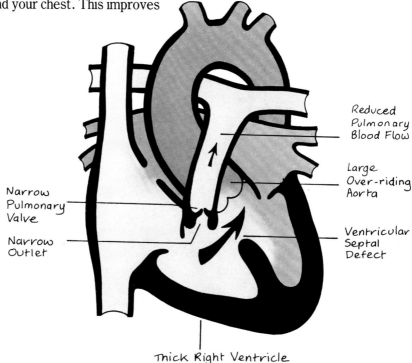

TETRALOGY OF FALLOT

53

TRICUSPID ATRESIA

The tricuspid valve is absent and the right ventricle is usually small There is a reduced blood flow to the lungs.

Blood has to pass from the right atrium into the left atrium, then into the left ventricle from which most of the blood will go to the body. Some blood will go through a hole in the ventricular septum into the small right ventricle and then into the lungs. These children usually present with blueness and murmurs early on in life, and occasionally spells like tetralogy of Fallot.

Increasing the blood flow to the lungs is necessary by a shunt procedure when symptoms warrant. This shunt procedure might need to be repeated as the years go by with growth.

Definitive surgery involves connecting the right atrium up to the lung arteries and closing the hole between the two receiving chambers. This is the Fontan procedure. For it to be successful it requires good sized lung arteries with low pressure within them, a good functioning left ventricle (main chamber) with no leaking of the mitral valve. This is a big operation, and the recovery period is slower than for other forms of cardiac surgery. Chest drains frequently need to be left in for a week or two as the body gets used to having a high pressure within the veins. There is gradual and continued improvement in wellbeing over many months after discharge. Medicines are usually required also for many months. Children frequently remain with a high colour with blue hands and feet and

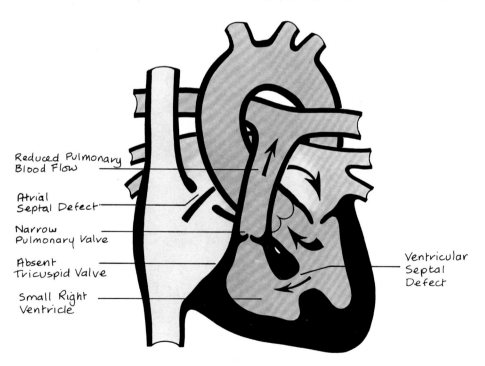

Reduced Pulmonary Blood Flow

Atrial Septal Defect

Narrow Pulmonary Valve

Absent Tricuspid Valve

Small Right Ventricle

Ventricular Septal Defect

TRUCUSPID ATRESIA

remain a little tired on strenuous exercise. Most, however, are able to play games at school and enjoy normal activities.

Antibiotic prophylaxis is required for life.

PULMONARY ATRESIA WITH NO VENTRICULAR SEPTAL DEFECT

In pulmonary atresia with intact ventricular septum, the pulmonary valve is blocked and blood flow to the lungs is dependent on the patency of the ductus. The right ventricle is of variable size and may be very small.

The babies usually present with blueness in the first days of life. Management depends on the size of the right ventricle. If it is small, it is unlikely to grow and a shunt procedure alone is necessary to take extra blood into the lungs. If the right ventricle is larger, then the pulmonary valve may be stretched or removed and a shunt undertaken. If the ventricle is almost of normal size, then the pulmonary valve may be just stretched or removed.

Further operations are often necessary to relieve residual obstruction or to overcome leaking in the area of the pulmonary valve. If the right ventricle is too small, the planned operation for the future would be a Fontan type operation connecting the right atrium up to the lung arteries.

Long term follow-up is necessary and antibiotic prophylaxis is life-long.

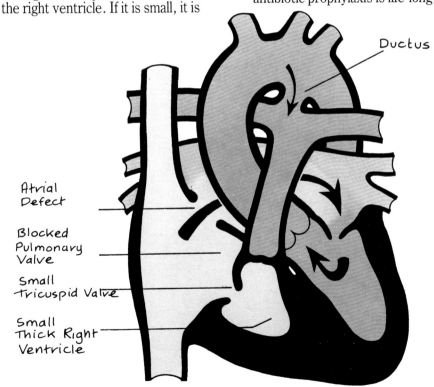

Ductus

Atrial Defect

Blocked Pulmonary Valve

Small Tricuspid Valve

Small Thick Right Ventricle

PULMONARY ATRESIA — INTACT VENTRICULAR SEPTUM

PULMONARY ATRESIA WITH VENTRICULAR SEPTAL DEFECT

There is complete blockage between the heart and the lung arteries, and a hole between the two pumping chambers. The right ventricle is of good size in this condition. Blood supply to the lungs may be from the ductus or from many fine collateral vessels. Detailed angiographic studies are required to look at the collateral vessels in order to plan the optimum management for each child. Many will require shunt procedures to increase the blood flow to the lungs. These shunts may be performed through the chest or through the breast bone. If the central lung arteries are of good size, then a repair joining the right ventricle to the lung artery can be undertaken later, either using a valved tube (conduit) or joining them directly with a patch. The hole between the two pumping chambers would be closed at the same time.

If the lung arteries are very small, then a series of shunts may be necessary. In some patients no operation is required as the condition is reasonably balanced. Long term follow-up is required and antibiotic prophylaxis is necessary for life.

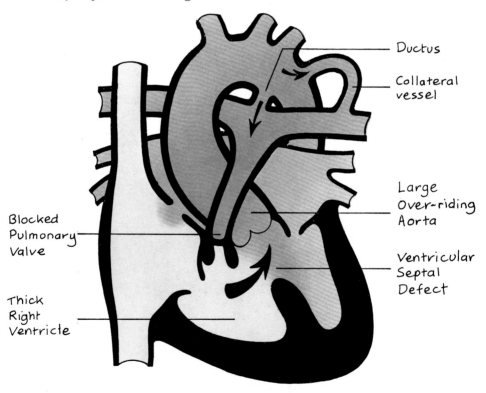

Ductus

Collateral vessel

Large Over-riding Aorta

Ventricular Septal Defect

Blocked Pulmonary Valve

Thick Right Ventricle

PULMONARY ATRESIA WITH VENTRICULAR SEPTAL DEFECT

SIMPLE TRANSPOSITION

The aorta arises from the right ventricle, and the pulmonary artery from the left ventricle. Deoxygenated blood is thus directed back to the body, and oxygenated blood from the lungs is directed back into the lungs.

These children present early in life with blueness. Usually a hole is made between the two receiving chambers of the heart by means of a catheter — a balloon septostomy. Many centres advise a repair to redirect blood flow through the atria (a Mustard or Senning procedure) during the first year of life. These procedures leave the left ventricle pumping to the lung artery and the right ventricle pumping to the body artery.

Other centres use the arterial switch operation to reimplant the arteries onto their normal ventricles. Both operations require 'open heart' surgery and are large operations. The arterial switch operation is undertaken in the first few weeks of life, and the atrial operation later in the first year.

Long term follow-up is required. Antibiotic prophylaxis will be life-long. The majority of children with both types of operation are well afterwards, and join in all normal activities.

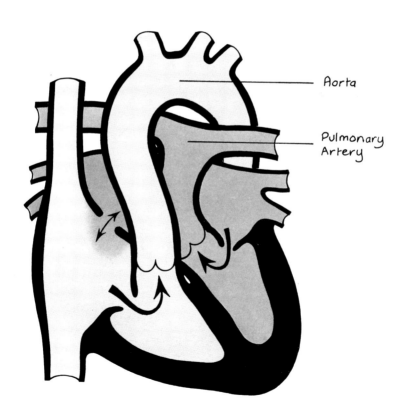

Aorta

Pulmonary Artery

SIMPLE TRANSPOSITION

COMPLEX TRANSPOSITION

1) Transposition with ventricular septal defect.
2) Transposition with patent ductus arteriosus

In both these conditions, there is a large communication between the two separate circulations. Despite this, most centres would advise making an additional hole between the two receiving chambers (balloon septostomy) by a catheter. The children are frequently only slightly blue but very breathless. They need medications to support their heart and require early surgery. This may involve narrowing the lung artery (banding), or repair of the defect. The repair may be switching the arteries back to normal and closing the communication, or redirection of blood within the atrium and closing the communication. Both repair operations are large operations requiring open heart surgery and usually need to be undertaken in the first months of life to prevent damage occurring to the lung arteries.

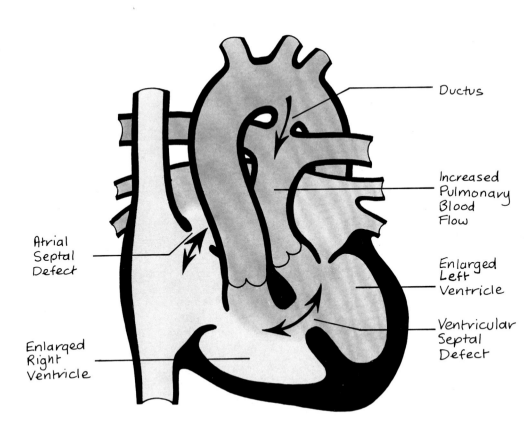

TRANSPOSITION WITH VENTRICULAR SEPTAL DEFECT.
PERSISTENT DUCTUS AND ATRIAL SEPTAL DEFECT.

3) Transposition with ventricular septal defect and pulmonary stenosis
The lungs are protected by the narrowing between the heart and the lung artery. The hole between the two pumping chambers allows the two streams of blood to mix, and therefore, these children are not as blue as those with simple transposition. However, as the months go by, the obstruction to blood flow increases, and a shunt procedure and enlarging of the atrial hole is frequently required. The obstruction between the heart and the lung arteries is difficult to relieve directly and usually has to be bypassed by a valved artificial tube (a conduit). This corrective operation is often postponed until the children are four to six years of age to allow an adequate sized tube to be inserted. This is a major operation requiring open heart surgery. Occasionally these tubes usually need further enlarging as the years go by. Antibiotic prophylaxis is life-long.

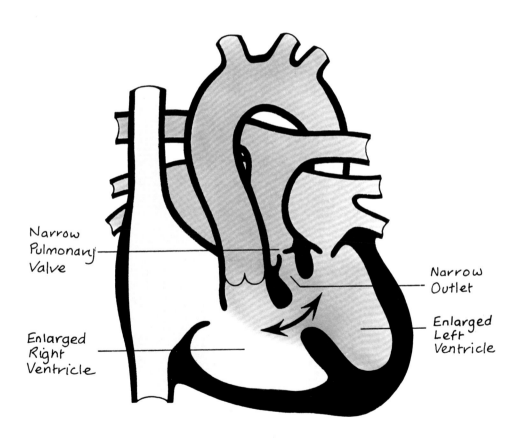

Narrow Pulmonary Valve

Enlarged Right Ventricle

Narrow Outlet

Enlarged Left Ventricle

TRANSPOSITION WITH VENTRICULAR SEPTAL DEFECT AND PULMONARY STENOSIS.

59

ATRIOVENTRICULAR SEPTAL DEFECT

In the partial form there is a hole between the two receiving chambers and an abnormal valve between the receiving chambers and the ventricles. In the complete form, this hole extends into the wall between the two pump chambers and there is one single valve between the two atria and the two ventricles. The hole allows excess blood to pass from the left to the right side of the heart. If the valve leaks , this increases the work of the heart by allowing blood to be pumped backwards into the receiving chambers as well as forwards into the arteries.

In the partial form, the children may be free of symptoms, unless the valve leaks significantly. In the complete form the children are frequently breathless, have difficulty with feeding, and poor weight gain in the first months of life. It is one of the commonest heart problems occurring in Down's syndrome.

Repair of the partial form involves patching the hole between the two receiving chambers and repairing the valve if it leaks. In the complete form the larger hole again is closed, the single valve is divided into two halves, and the middle portions of the valves are attached to the patch. This is a major operation and needs to be done early in life before damage to the lungs occurs. In some children narrowing of the lung artery, a banding, may be planned in the first instance to protect the lungs and allow the child go grow.

Long term follow-up is required. The majority of children are significantly improved as a result of their surgery. Residual leaking of repaired valves can be a problem and if severe, further surgery may be necessary. Antibiotic prophylaxis is necessary life-long.

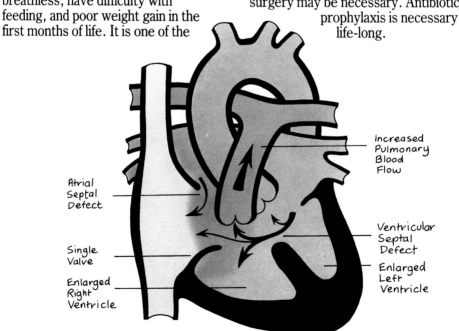

Atrial Septal Defect

Single Valve

Enlarged Right Ventricle

Increased Pulmonary Blood Flow

Ventricular Septal Defect

Enlarged Left Ventricle

COMPLETE ATRIO-VENTRICULAR SEPTAL DEFECT

ANOMALOUS PULMONARY VENOUS DRAINAGE

The pulmonary veins instead of connecting into the left atrium connect into the right side of the circulation. If only some of the veins drain abnormally the term 'partial' is used, if all of them drain abnormally it is described as 'total'. There are several sites into which the veins may drain. These are shown in the diagram and may be above the heart into the large veins (1 or 2), within the heart either into the right atrium or coronary sinus (3 or 4); or below the heart into the liver or into the major lower vein (5).

If the connection is narrow (obstructed) then the child will present in the early days of life with blueness and breathlessness because blood has difficulty in returning from the lungs into the heart. If the connection is wide open (non-obstructed) then the problems are breathlessness, chest infections and poor weight gain and come to light during the first year of life rather than the first few days.

Open heart surgery to redirect the blood flow back into the left atrium is required when symptoms (complaints) occur.

Although the operation is a complex one and initial recovery is slow, the long term outlook is very good.

Antibiotic prophylaxis is required for life.

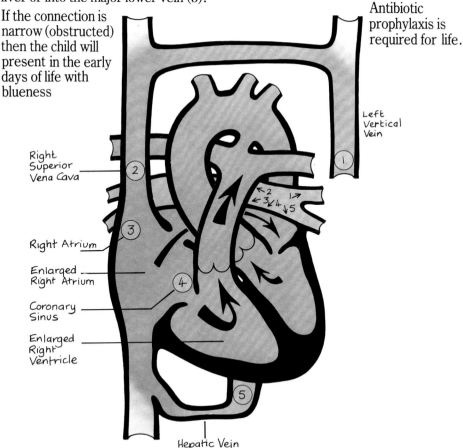

Left Vertical Vein

Right Superior Vena Cava

Right Atrium

Enlarged Right Atrium

Coronary Sinus

Enlarged Right Ventricle

Hepatic Vein

TOTAL ANOMALOUS PULMONARY VENOUS DRAINAGE

DOUBLE INLET VENTRICLE

In this group of conditions there is a large pumping chamber (ventricle) into which both atria empty their blood through either one or two valves. There is usually a second smaller pump chamber at the side of the main ventricle. The arteries commonly come one from each ventricle as in the diagram, or both may arise from one of the ventricles.

If there is no additional narrowing to flow of blood into the lungs the children will be breathless, feed poorly and gain weight slowly. Often narrowing (banding) of the lung artery will be required in the first instance. If there is severe obstruction of blood flow to the lungs, then the child will be blue and may require the blood supply to the lungs to be increased with a shunt operation.

Some children are very nicely balanced; not too breathless and not too blue.

Many children can be improved very significantly by these minor operations. Others require or are suitable for further help. In some cases it is possible to divide the ventricle into two working halves by a large patch. This is called 'septation'.

More frequently the Fontan type operation connecting the large veins from the body directly to the lung artery is performed. This leaves both the main ventricle and the smaller ventricle pumping blood to the body.

Both these types of operation are major operations requiring open heart surgery.

Antibiotic prophylaxis is required for life.

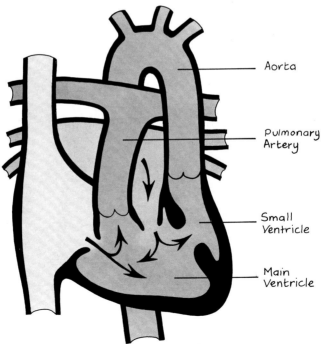

Aorta

Pulmonary Artery

Small Ventricle

Main Ventricle

DOUBLE INLET VENTRICLE

TRUNCUS ARTERIOSUS

There is one large single artery arising from the heart which then divides into the lung artery and the body artery. There is, in addition, a large hole between the two pumping chambers. This problem allows a very high blood flow to the lungs, which makes the child breathless, liable to repeated infections, and to gain weight poorly. Initially, help is given with medicines, but an operation to repair the problem is necessary within the first months of life. This involves closing the hole between the pumping chambers, and taking the lung artery off the side of the body artery, connecting it with a conduit (a tube) to the right ventricle. The operation needs to be performed before the lung arteries are damaged by the high blood flow and a high pressure. This is a large operation and the conduit will need to be replaced as the child grows in due course.

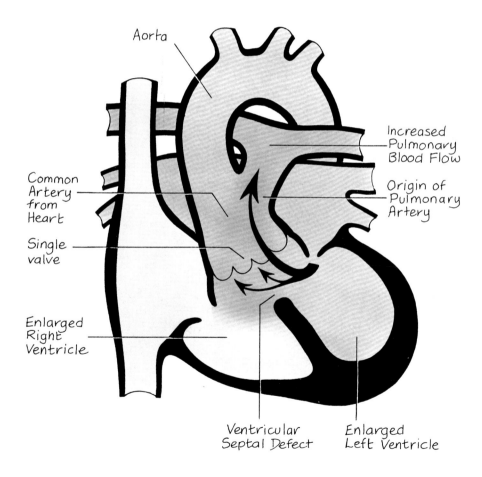

TRUNCUS ARTERIOSUS

CARDIOMYOPATHY
1 DILATED CARDIOMYOPATHY

In this condition the muscle of the heart is weak and the heart usually enlarged. Children present with feeding difficulties, breathlessness, poor weight gain and recurrent chest infections. The cause in many is unknown. In some it may be related to previous viral infections.

Medications are often required long term. These make the heart work more efficiently and remove excess fluid. Most children gradually improve. In some, the damage to the heart muscle is more severe and their condition gets worse. If this happens, despite large doses of many medicines, then heart transplantation may be considered.

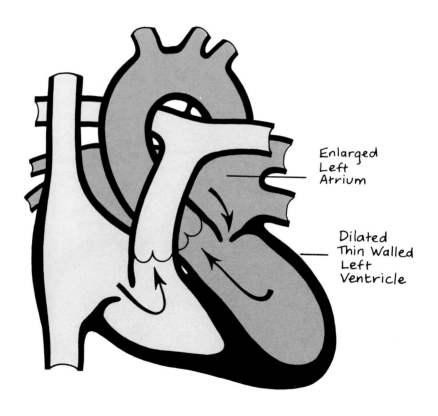

Enlarged Left Atrium

Dilated Thin Walled Left Ventricle

DILATED CARDIOMYOPATHY

2 HYPERTROPHIC CARDIOMYOPATHY

The heart muscle is very thick and has difficulty in relaxing. Sometimes the extra muscle causes obstruction to blood flow out of the heart. Many cases are mild with no symptoms, others have dizziness, fainting attacks palpitations and chest discomfort.

Regular drugs are used if symptoms are present and these help improve relaxation of the heart muscle and control abnormalities of heart rhythm. Long term follow-up is necessary. Antibiotic prophylaxis is also necessary life-long.

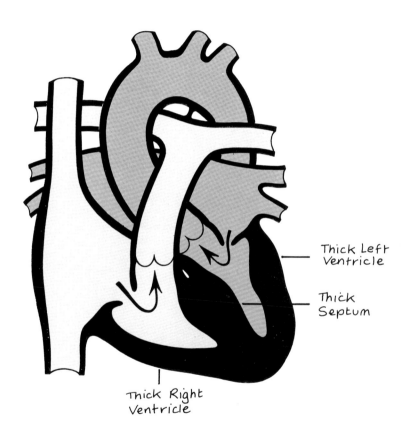

Thick Left Ventricle

Thick Septum

Thick Right Ventricle

HYPERTROPHIC CARDIOMYOPATHY

HYPOPLASTIC LEFT HEART SYNDROME

The main pumping chamber (the left ventricle) is very small and the aortic and mitral valves are either very narrow, thickened or entirely blocked. The babies are in major difficulties in the first few days of life as changes in the circulation occur with closure of the ductus. Many doctors feel that intervention is not feasible and the majority of the babies die peacefully very early in life. Some recommend early transplantation, although donors are scarce, whilst others have attempted major high risk surgery early in life. This is open heart surgery and involves joining the small aorta to the start of the large lung artery, dividing the branches of the lung artery and connecting these to a shunt from the aorta. In addition the hole between the receiving chambers is enlarged. This is a very big operation. Some of those who come through it would be suitable for a Fontan type operation joining the receiving chamber on the right side of the heart up directly to the lung artery; for others the only hope would be heart transplantation in due course.

This is a difficult area and each unit will have discussed very carefully its own policy for these children with such severe problems.

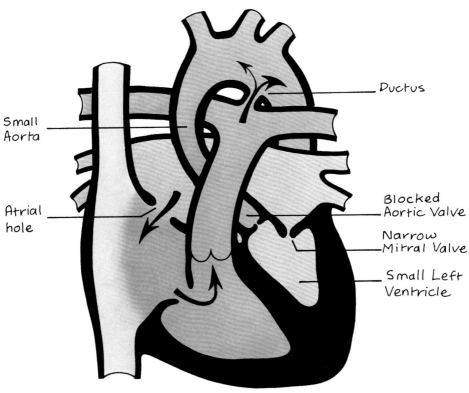

HYPOPLASTIC LEFT HEART

PERSISTENT FETAL CIRCULATION

The heart and lungs themselves are formed normally, but the lung arteries in both lungs remain narrow and constricted as they are in the womb. As a result of this, the pressure in the lung artery remains very high and de-oxygenated blood is directed across the small flap valve between the atria and also across the ductus between the arteries.

It is often difficult to differentiate this condition from structural heart problems and babies are thus often referred to Cardiac Units.

The management consists of ventilation and medicines to try and open up the narrow lung arteries. In some patients the arteries open quickly and the condition improves. In others the arteries do not open up and the child's condition can be very critical for long periods of time and sometimes the child may not survive. The cause for this particular problem is unknown.

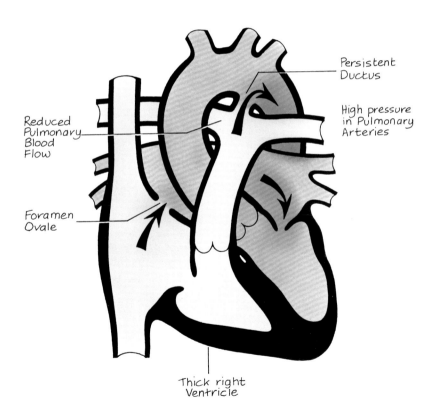

PERSISTENT FETAL CIRCULATION

11 FUNDAMENTAL FACTS for parents about children's heart problems

HEART FAILURE

This is the term used when the pumping action of the heart is insufficient to meet the needs of the body. It means that the heart muscle has extra work to do and help is often needed with medicines and sometimes operations.

It is one of the common presentations of heart problems in children. It is important to reassure everyone that it does not mean that the heart is going to stop or that a serious collapse is likely to occur. However there are different degrees of heart failure ranging from mild to severe.

There are many causes of this extra work and they can occur on their own or in combination with each other. Common examples are large holes between the two sides of the heart, significantly narrow or leaking valves, or weak heart muscle. As a result extra fluid and salts are retained in the body making the lungs wetter, heavier and stiffer than normal causing breathlessness. In small babies and children feeding is frequently difficult with slow weight gain and frequent chest infections. In the older child tiredness and increasing breathlessness on exercise occur. Sometimes the extra fluid produces abdominal discomfort and swelling and occasionally a puffy face.

TREATMENT — These children can be greatly helped by medicines and depending on the cause may need an operation.

ENDOCARDITIS

This is an infection ('ITIS') of the endocardium, which is the smooth lining of the heart. It is extremely rare in normal hearts, and is even uncommon in those that are abnormal. In conditions where there is an abnormal blood flow in the heart, turbulence occurs. This causes some localized thickening and roughening of the lining layer. If bacteria get into the blood stream in large quantities, they may land in the crevices of this rough area and cause an infection. This produces general effects such as tiredness, lethargy, fever, weight loss and sweating, and local effects by damage to the area of the infection, particularly relating to the heart valves. In addition, small clots of blood, which may form on the infected areas, can fly off into the circulation and produce problems. Endocarditis is extremely rare in pulmonary stenosis and atrial septal defects, but is relatively more common in aortic stenosis, mitral incompetence, ventricular septal defects and persistent ductus arteriosus.

Management involves confirming the diagnosis usually by taking repeated blood tests to look for the bacteria, and then giving large doses of powerful antibiotics, usually into one of the veins for a long period of time (between three to six weeks). During much of this time the child will need to be in hospital. The majority of children make a slow recovery. However, occasionally the infection does not clear and the possibility of urgent surgery may need to be considered. This is a serious illness and any procedures which are known to be associated with bacteria getting in the blood stream should be covered by giving the patient a large dose of antibiotics beforehand. Most units have cards which they give to parents to show to local doctors and dentists.

ARRHYTHMIAS

This is a general term for an abnormal heart rhythm. This may occur as an isolated problem when the heart is otherwise normal, or in addition to an underlying structural problem.

Extra beats interposed between normal beats are very common and may produce extra thumps. These are benign and strong reassurance is all that is necessary.

If the heart rate is relatively slow, termed bradycardia, often there are no symptoms, the circulation in the heart working rather like that of an athlete. If complaints do occur such as dizziness, lightheadedness, tiredness, then a pacemaker may be needed. If the heart rate is too fast, this is called tachycardia. These fast rhythms can occur either from above the ventricles (supraventricular) or from the ventricles themselves (ventricular). If the episodes of fast beating are infrequent, then often no regular medicines are required. Many children learn tricks that are able to slow the fast rate or stop it. Ones that are frequently successful are slow, but deep breathing; trying to make your ears pop, by taking a deep breath in, pinching your nose, closing your lips tightly and trying to blow out; a cold fizzy drink; making oneself gag by putting a finger on the back of the tongue. If the episodes are more

frequent or cause the child to feel unwell, then regular medications may be required. These are used to reduce the chance of the episodes occurring and also to reduce the speed at which the heart responds. The type of medicine and the length of treatment vary greatly. Very occasionally if the symptoms are very troublesome and the response to medicine poor, then an open heart operation may be recommended to remove that small area of heart muscle that is causing the arrhythmia.

PACEMAKER

If the heart rate becomes too slow to meet the usual demands of the body complaints occur such as dizziness, lightheadedness, tiredness and breathlessness. If this is the case and is confirmed by tests, then the heart's action needs to be speeded up. Usually this needs to be performed artificially by a pacemaker.

The insertion of such a pacemaker may also be recommended if the chances of a sudden reduction in heart rate are felt to be high after some types of complex cardiac surgery.

A pacemaker consists of a battery and a complex electric circuit which controls its power. It weighs about 4oz and is about the size of a matchbox. The battery can be implanted under the skin and connected by a fine wire either to the outside of the heart (the epicardium) or to the inside of the heart (the endocardium) using a vein. With the epicardial type, the wire is sewn on to the outside of the heart by an operation. With the endocardial, the fine wire is inserted through a vein and steered into the heart under X-ray control in a catheter laboratory.

Most pacemakers are programmable; that is the rate, power supply and timing can be altered externally after the pacemaker has been inserted. This can be done with an electromagnetic 'programmer'. These alterations allow the optimum pacing settings to be obtained for each individual child.

Some of the new pacemakers are termed 'physiological'. This means that they can alter the rate of pacing in response to exercise. These can be particularly useful in the older children.

Techniques and technology have improved very considerably over the past five years, and the majority of pacing systems now inserted will hopefully last for more than ten years. At that stage the pacing box containing its batteries would need to be removed and replaced by a new one. Hopefully, the wire connecting the battery to the heart would not need to be replaced.

Regular follow-up with checking of the pacemaker is required.

There is very little interference from outside electrical circuits but strong electrical fields such as occur with 'dodgem' cars at the fairground or arc welding should be avoided. Most

occupations and activities can be undertaken. Ordinary driving licences may be held but not those for heavy goods vehicles.

OPEN HEART SURGERY

This term is used to describe operations on the heart and major blood vessels when the heart's action is stopped. The blood supply to the body is maintained by an artificial pump and oxygenator — the heart/lung machine. This is connected to the veins and arteries by a set of tubes and maintains the blood supply to the body while the operation on the heart is being undertaken. The body's temperature is frequently cooled (hypothermia) to reduce the demands of the body and a special salt solution (cardioplegia) is used to protect the heart muscle.

The children are anaesthetised, have several fine tubes inserted into the large veins, often in the neck, to be able to measure pressures within the veins and to give drugs. A line is placed in an artery, usually in the arm or sometimes the leg to measure the

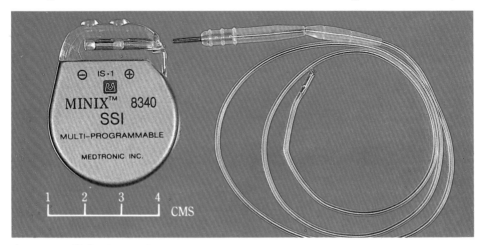

A programmable heart pacemaker

70

blood pressure. The operations are usually carried out through the breast bone (sternum) and take between three and five hours depending on the complexity. The heart/lung machine and its tubes are connected to the patient, maintaining the blood supply to the body and the heart is relaxed. The heart chamber or vessel is then opened, the defect repaired and following this the walls sewn up. The heart is then stimulated and takes over the circulation and gradually the bypass machine can be withdrawn.

Additional tubes (drains) are left around the heart to ensure that any excess fluid is removed, and frequently fine pacing wires are sewn onto the front surface of the heart. Through these an electrical current can be given to increase the heart rate if the patient's own rate is a bit slow.

On return to the ward, most children will still require help with their breathing with the aid of a ventilator and will have the small tubes coming out of their chest to allow the fluid to drain away.

Over the next hours and days these will gradually be removed and the child will leave Intensive Care. Many children will need to take several medications following their discharge from hospital. This is routine practice. Frequently over the subsequent weeks and months these will be able to be reduced following review in Out-patients.

CLOSED SURGERY

This describes operations where the heart's action is not stopped. These are often undertaken through the side of the chest. Repair of coarctation, ligation of the ductus, banding of the lung artery to reduce excessive blood flow stretching of pulmonary and aortic valves and shunt procedures to increase the blood flow into the lungs are examples of closed surgery.

The children are anaesthetised, frequently have drips in the side of the neck or the arm; a small tube is often put in an artery to measure the pressure. The incision usually is under the arm running along the line of the ribs. The underlying lung is moved to one side and the defect repaired or a shunt created. The lung is allowed to move back. A small tube is inserted into the chest to allow air and fluid to drain out and to ensure that the lung expands fully. On return to the ward the children may be ventilated, particularly if they are young.

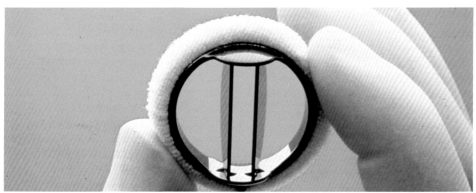

A St. Jude artificial heart valve

Occasionally closed surgery is undertaken through the breast bone when the blood flow coming into the heart can be reduced allowing straight forward procedures to be undertaken. This is called inflow occlusion.

VALVE REPLACEMENT

If a valve is very abnormal, repair may not be possible and the valve would need to be replaced. There are different types of these new valves that are best in different positions, and as the years go by, this choice will change. Artificial valves will not grow with the child and may need replacing as growth occurs over the years. The largest possible valve is therefore inserted at the first operation. All these operations require open heart surgery. The size of the valve used in children and in young adults has caused no problems with valve failure and strut fractures.

In the mitral position, the usual valve used is a metal and plastic valve, for example a Bjork Shiley or St Jude. Their drawback is that the blood needs to be thinned with anticoagulants to prevent small clots developing on the valve. These may fly off into the circulation or cause the valve to stick or leak. The degree of blood thinning needs to be checked by regular tests.

The aortic valve can be replaced by a similar sort of valve. It may, however, be possible to replace it by another human valve (a homograft). This avoids the use of anticoagulants, which is particularly beneficial in children and young women.

The tricuspid valve may require replacement with a plastic and metal valve. Occasionally a homograft may be used. Rarely the valve may be removed altogether without the need to replace it.

In contrast a pulmonary valve that is so abnormal may be removed completely and the right-sided pump chamber copes very well with the modest degree of extra work that the leak of blood back from the lungs produces.

Occasionally this leak is excessive and a pulmonary valve would need to be inserted. This usually is a homograft and can be sewn on to the top of the right ventricle.

A valve replacement is a more major undertaking in children than in adults. It requires enough space within the heart to insert the valve. Regular long term follow-up is required and antibiotic prophylaxis is very important.

CONDUIT

A conduit is an artificial tube that carries blood, and usually has a valve within it. The use of conduits has made previously inoperable heart disease treatable. The valve may be a homograft (another human valve) or a xenograft (pig or calf valve). Conduits are used when it is impossible to repair a valve, to replace a valve when it is completely missing — or to bypass a severe narrowing that cannot be relieved directly.

The valve and conduit will not grow and if they need to be inserted in small children will have to be replaced as the years go by. Many of the conduit operations are postponed until the child is between four and eight years when a large size can be used. However, even then some of these will require a further operation because of the development of narrowing over many years.

Long term follow up is required, as is antibiotic propylaxis.

Transplantation: Heart, Heart and Lung, Lung

Heart transplantations were first performed in adults in the late 1960s. Because of problems with rejection, the numbers of patients were very small until the late 1970s. Then, as a result of research largely from Stanford in California, with better methods of detecting rejection and improved drugs to combat the rejection, the number of transplants undertaken has increased very markedly and the results improved. With the advent of Cyclosporin as a major drug to combat rejection of the new heart, much lower doses of steroids need to be used. The combination of this drug and the improving results in adults have now made transplantation available to children.

Transplantation may be offered to patients when their heart or lung problems are very serious and their condition is deteriorating. If the problem is only the heart and the lungs are good then only the heart is transplanted. If the lungs are badly damaged, either by infection – such as occurs in cystic fibrosis – or because of abnormal lung blood vessels (high blood pressure or severe narrowing) both heart and lungs are transplanted. If the lung problem relates to scarring without significant infection then transplantation of one lung alone may be used. Transplantation operations may not be carried out in all cardiac centres and therefore the children and families would need to meet and be assessed by the transplant team. This gives everyone a chance to meet a new

'. . . I couldn't do this before!'

team of doctors, nurses, technicians and social worker, who are involved in the operation and the care afterwards. During this assessment time they will meet others who have had transplants and learn about the difficulties, problems and implications of having this sort of treatment.

The waiting time for the actual transplant is very variable as the supply of new hearts and lungs is unpredictable. In addition the team have to match up not only size but blood group. This waiting often causes a great strain on all members of the family.

When a suitable organ is available the family are told and have to return to the transplant unit as soon as possible. Good planning by all is necessary for this to take place. The operation lasts from four to six hours and it very frequently happens at weekends or at night. The child will usually return to a special ward in order to reduce the chance of infection immediately after surgery.

The main problems after transplantation are suppressing the body's attempts to reject the new organs and preventing infection. To do this several powerful drugs are used and in the first days after the operation these are given in very high doses.

changes, breathing tests, sound wave tests and also by taking small pieces of heart muscle or lung tissue and looking at them under the microscope (biopsies). Infection is detected by temperature changes and tests on blood, urine, sputum etc.

The long term results from transplantation in children are not yet known. The child will need to take medicines life long to damp down the body's attempts to reject the new organs. Side-effects may be a problem with the medicines and blood tests need to be performed fairly regularly to check that the doses are appropriate.

Transplantation is thus a very major step. The family and the child need to be aware of the difficulties associated with it. It can, however, mean a significantly improved quality of life for children with very severe problems.

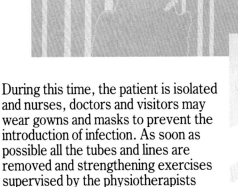

During this time, the patient is isolated and nurses, doctors and visitors may wear gowns and masks to prevent the introduction of infection. As soon as possible all the tubes and lines are removed and strengthening exercises supervised by the physiotherapists start very early. Over the next days and weeks the optimum doses of the anti-rejection drugs are worked out for each individual patient.

Rejection occurs in almost all patients at some stage or another — most frequently within the first few weeks. Rejection is assessed by temperature

'Before . . . and after my transplant operation.' These vivid computer illustrations done in hospital by a young patient, say it all.

CHAPTER

12 STATE BENEFITS AND SUPPORT SERVICES

A child with a heart condition can mean extra expense for a family, e.g. for hospital admission, fares for hospital appointments, higher heating costs etc. Many people may not realise that they can get some financial help from the state benefit system. Here are some of the ways that you may be able to get assistance.

The State Benefit system is very complicated. The rate of unemployment and the high cost of living means that quite a number of families these days are eligible to receive some state benefits.

All families receive **Child Benefit** and some may also be receiving **Family Credit**. The weekly needs of claimants are now assessed differently and the long term rate or additions for special needs such as heating have gone. In the new legislation each claimant gets a basic personal allowance (lower rate for single persons under 25). There are then flat rate premiums for specific categories of claimant, i.e. disabled, single parents and families with children.

If a couple have a child who counts as disabled, i.e. receiving **Attendance Allowance** and or **Mobility Allowance** they can receive an additional **Disabled Child Premium** which is at present £16.65 per week. (April 1991 rate).

All families in receipt of **Income Support** or **Family Credit** will automatically be entitled to free NHS dental treatment, vouchers for glasses, free NHS prescriptions and refund of travel costs to hospital for NHS treatment.

Even if you are not entitled to Family Credit or Income Support, but are on a low income get Form AG1, **'Help With NHS Costs'** from a Social Security Office, hospital, dentist or optician. Complete it and send to:

Agency Benefits Unit
DSS
Longbenton
Newcastle-upon-Tyne
NE98 1YX.

They will check your circumstances and if you are entitled to any help you will be sent a certificate of entitlement which you can use to claim refunds. The certificate lasts for six months and is not affected if your earnings increase during that time.

Your claim can include public transport fares, petrol costs or taxi fares (if this is the only way your child can travel). However, the claim only covers taking a child to and from hospital, it does not help with visiting fares. If you do get Family Credit or Income Support you can claim travel costs to and from hospital by producing your order book or other proof of benefit payments at the hospital. If there are any problems, then ask to speak to the hospital social worker. Fares to help families visit children in hospital might be claimed via a **Community Care Grant**. This is a cash grant (not repayable) available on a discretionary basis. For details write to your Social Security Office and ask for Form SF300.

ATTENDANCE ALLOWANCE

Some families are eligible for Attendance Allowance for their children if the child's disability means that they need constant care. This benefit is not means tested.

They are eligible if their child or baby has needed constant care for the previous six months. Use the claim form in Claim Pack DS2 which is available from your local DSS office, Citizens Advice Bureau, whose address is in the front of your Thomson Directory, or Heart Line office (see address on page 86).

For day or night time care only, you would get £27.80 per week and for both day **and** night care £41.65 per week. (April 1991 rates).

INVALID CARE ALLOWANCE

If your child gets Attendance Allowance and you cannot go out to work because you are caring for your child you may be able to get Invalid Care Allowance. You must be caring for the child for at least 35 hours a week and earning not more than £30 a week after deductions. Invalid Care Allowance is currently £31.25 per week (April 1991 rate). It is important to remember, though that if you are claiming Income Support this will be reduced by the amount of your Invalid Care Allowance.

There are, however, hidden advantages in claiming Invalid Care Allowance, even if the family income remains the same, because it is taken into account as income for means tested benefits. This means that if you get Invalid Care Allowance you may also get the £10 Christmas bonus and also an extra £10.80 per week is included in any assessment for Income Support, housing benefit etc.

MOBILITY ALLOWANCE

If your child has difficulty in walking or cannot walk at all and is over 5 years of age, then you can claim Mobility Allowance for the extra cost in getting about.

This is another non means tested benefit. Use Form N1211 to claim. The current rate is £29.10 per week (April 1991).

You may also be exempt from road tax if you have a car and it is used for the sole purpose of transporting your disabled child. If you think that you may qualify for exemption from road tax write to the Mobility Allowance Unit from where your payment book comes.

SEVERE DISABLEMENT ALLOWANCE

When your child becomes sixteen, if he is incapable of work because of his disability he may be entitled to Severe Disablement Allowance. A child aged between 16 and 19 years who is incapable of work, but who is in full time education, may get Severe Disablement Allowance if the course he attends is for less than 21 hours per week or the course is deemed unsuitable for a person of the same age who is not disabled.

The amount of Severe Disablement Allowance depends on the age at which a person becomes incapable of work. The current weekly rate is £42.35 for someone who became incapable of work before their 40th birthday. (April 1991 rate).

Use the claim form on leaflet NI252, which also gives more information.

The DSS produce a guide to benefits means tested and other, called 'Which Benefit'. Leaflet FB2.

Leaflet NI196 Social Security Benefit Rates provides up to date benefit rates, earnings rules etc.

Copies of these are available from your local DSS office or from the Heart Line office (See page 86 for address).

For general information you can also phone the DSS on their Freephone National Hotline: 0800 882200.

The Child Poverty Action Group publish two very useful books annually. These are called The National Welfare Benefits Handbook and Rights Guide to non-means-tested benefits. These books are available from Child Poverty Action Group, 4th Floor, 1-5 Bath Street, London, EC1V 9PY.

A copy of these books is also available in the Heart Line office. They will help you find your way around the State Benefit System and are not difficult to understand.

OTHER FINANCIAL SUPPORT

People on Income Support or a low income can sometimes get additional help from various organisations for specific things e.g. help with hospital expenses, help to buy a spin dryer, or to have a holiday if they have a sick child, or are themselves disabled, or for any reason where the stress in the family can be judged to be greater than average.

Various associations help in situations like this, for example, the Chest, Heart and Stroke Association or the Family Fund for sick and disabled children. Apply to the former through a health visitor or social worker. The latter you can contact directly yourself. The Fund will usually send their own Social Worker to assess your individual needs. They are sympathetic towards help required for driving lessons e.g.

to get your child to and from hospital, doctors etc., the installation of telephones, or providing for specific needs of that child including help with holidays.

Some professions, like the Forces, the Civil Service and several others, have their own funds and will consider applications from families. You can apply directly to the funds themselves, or ask your health visitor or social worker to apply.

The Citizens Advice Bureau may be able to give you advice about local trusts. Sometimes Public Libraries also have information about local charities. Lions Clubs and Rotary Clubs might also give families help. Several other associations may give families financial help or holidays for a family, for example 'Break' in Sheringham, Norfolk; the Church of England Children's Society, London; The Jewish Welfare Board; The Lady Haw Trust for Physically Disabled Children in Midhurst, West Sussex. Heart Line also has two holiday caravans for use by families, one based in Skegness and one in Selsey.

It is not possible to give a list of all organisations offering help in the UK, but Heart Line and other support groups may be able to supply a more extensive list or help with specific problems, on request (see pages 86 and 87 for contact addresses.

TRAVEL

Trains – A person who is registered disabled may get half price travel for himself and one accompanying adult if he has a railcard. You may be eligible; ask British Rail for a leaflet.

Taxis – If you live in London and receive Mobility Allowance, or your doctor certifies by letter that you or your child are unable to use public transport because of a disability that seriously affects your walking ability, you can get a Taxicard which enables you to make a journey of up to £9 in the Greater London Area for only £1.25.

Ask your Post Office for a form. The hospital social services department should also keep these forms.

The Department of Transport produce a booklet called 'Door to Door' which covers all aspects of transport for disabled travellers.

Other practical information

THE FAMILY

The family may be under a lot of stress if your child is ill. Remember that it might help to talk to your health visitor or GP. You could also contact your local social worker. This sort of support may be particularly helpful for the single parent who is isolated from parents and friends.

Social Services can sometimes arrange for a Home Aid or Home Help to come to the house on a short term basis when the family is in the middle of a crisis and is finding it difficult to cope. They may also know of any local parent support groups.

Community workers, like social workers and health visitors, will also know of any special playgroups or nurseries or other facilities that might be available for a child with a heart condition, to help the child and to relieve the other members of the family from this extra stress.

WORK

If a child goes into hospital, sometimes a father may have to take time off work to help take care of the rest of the family, or may be in hospital with the child. While some employers are sympathetic and grant compassionate leave, others may be less understanding and fathers may end up receiving no pay.

It may well help to get the hospital social worker to contact your work and discuss the problem with them: sometimes employers really do not realise the implications of long term hospital stays or repeated outpatients appointments.

However, if no pay is granted, parents may then need advice and help about applying for Income Support. Self-employed fathers are particularly vulnerable in this situation and may well find that the benefit they receive is small. Consult your hospital social worker again about this.

STATE HOUSING

Sometimes home conditions are such that they are detrimental to the child: for example if there are a lot of stairs and no lift and the child's condition limits his physical ability or the accommodation is damp and/or there is inadequate heating. Generally in situations like this, a medical letter can be sent to the Housing Department supporting a housing transfer request. This may speed things up but it will vary from area to area according to local need. Sometimes medical staff will support a re-housing request which is not directly detrimental — if the child has multiple disabilities, eg the doctors may think that poor housing is an added stress from which the parents need to be removed.

HOUSING ALTERATIONS
For disabled children, eg showers, downstairs lavatories, alterations for wheelchairs: you may be eligible for a grant for this. Contact your Occupational Therapist at your local Social Services Department. The grant can be up to 80% of the total cost depending on area.

RATES
Rates may rise if you improve your home, but if the disabled person is registered as disabled, this should be waived.

PUSHCHAIRS/BUGGIES
If your child's heart condition limits him considerably, you may need a larger, strong pushchair or buggy when he gets older.

You can get the large strong pushchair called the 'MacLaren Major Buggy' from several sources — through your GP or health visitor, or contact your District Health Authority or hospital.

Your nearest Artificial Limb and Appliance Centre (in the telephone book under Health and Social Security — Department of) will also be able to help you.

ORANGE BADGE SCHEME
A disabled family member entitles you to park your car in some no parking areas. Ask your Social Services Department about this

WORK
If your child has left school and wants to start to look for work and is registered as disabled, contact the DRO (Disablement Resettlement Officer) at your local Job Centre.

SIGNING-ON RULES
It might be useful for parents to know when signing on for work, rules for the unemployed can be waived at the discretion of the Benefit Officer.

This is waived in special circumstances eg if a parent is staying in a hospital away from home with a child who is temporarily ill, and either the other parent who normally looks after the child is unable to do so, or if there is no other parent.

This regulation comes under Supplementary Benefit Conditions of the Entitlement Regulations 1981 No 1525 Regulation 6.

EDUCATION
The 1981 Education Act states that all school children have a right to education and therefore it is the statutory duty of the Education Authorities to see that they receive it.

Sometimes education really is a problem, if the child is too unwell to go to school, or physically unable to cope with the journey or move about school. It can be difficult if the school is large, on several different levels or your child has to go out of doors to get to some classrooms. These things are worth checking before he begins at a new school. With a little imagination it may be possible to juggle the school timetable slightly so that a child with a heart problem, or indeed any physical disability, does not have to expend energy needlessly to reach classrooms spaced a long way apart. After surgery, a child may have a period of time away from school and it may be necessary to arrange home tuition. If you think this is going to be necessary, get in touch with your local Education Department in plenty of time as these things do take a while to sort out.

ABOUT 'STATEMENTING'

If your child's problems are severe, the school may feel that he would benefit from the help of a Welfare Assistant. Then it may be necessary to have your child 'statemented' as having special needs. Many parents worry about this procedure and fear that their child will be 'singled out' or that a school will not wish to take their child if he has 'special needs'. It is important to be aware that your wishes as a parent are considered paramount. You are encouraged (in some places, required) to send in your own view of your child's needs so that these can be taken into account with all the rest when a decision is made about whether to grant a helper or not. Statementing does *not* mean that your child will be whisked off to a different school. Quite the reverse in fact, most schools welcome a statemented child, particularly if he has been granted a welfare assistant. Since it is normally undesirable for the assistant to be continually hovering over that child it means that an extra pair of hands is often available in the classroom for the benefit of all the children in that class.

CHAPTER

13 BEREAVEMENT

At some time in the lives of children with severe heart defects, most have periods of being 'on the critical list'. For the majority, these periods are mercifully short-lived and the trauma quickly forgotten in the happiness of recovery. There are occasions however, when children die. This is devastating for the parents and relatives and deeply upsetting for the medical/nursing team, who expend so much effort in prolonging life. When a child remains critically ill, no-one knows exactly what to do or say.

Many parents in this situation are aware of feeling alienated from nursing staff and other parents in the unit. They desperately want to know exactly what is happening to their child but are terrified of hearing the worst. Staff tend, to some extent, to follow the lead given by the parents and so develops what, to some parents, seems to amount to a conspiracy of silence. There is no completely satisfactory way of over-coming this problem.

Death is not a subject which we in this country are encouraged to discuss. Parents may be afraid of appearing morbid if they ask if their child is going to die, and medical staff will not bring it up for fear of upsetting the parents. At the same time it is the one thing which is on everyone's minds. Not being able to voice this almost immobilising fear adds to the strain. Many parents also feel that they cannot mention the word 'dying' when their child is still fighting to live.

The grief which occurs as a result of bereavement has been described as 'a reaction in which normal functioning no longer holds'. In fact, many bereaved parents talk of feeling as though 'they are going mad', they worry about coping with the intensity of their feelings and find the rapid changes which their emotions go through very bewildering.

If you have suffered a bereavement, or you are supporting parents who have, this chapter has been written in the hope that it may help for you to know that these swinging changes in mood are normal. No-one who has not been through the loss of a child of their own can really understand what you are experiencing.

One of the worst aspects of loss that parents describe is the total inability to do anything about what has happened. Most things that occur in our lives we have some control over, or we can do something to ease the situation. There is nothing one can do to change the death of a child. Often it is the sense of helplessness that this knowledge brings that adds to the feelings of anger and pain.

THE PROCESS OF GRIEVING

It is generally believed that there are three main stages of grief, and that these have to be worked through — but the order and timing of each part of the stages does vary with each individual.

Briefly, the stages are:- **shock and numbness**, these are the **initial reactions** to loss and may include actual physical symptoms of palpitations, muscular weakness or nausea. The numbness makes our surroundings seem unreal and remote, as though we are distanced from what is happening. Another aspect of this first stage is a denial of what has happened. Parents temporarily 'forget' their loss and find themselves laying their child's place at the table for example, running their bath or buying an item of clothing while out shopping. This temporary denial of reality is also perfectly normal.

The second stage is a gradual realisation of what has happened and this is accompanied by rapidly changing feelings of anger, apathy, exhaustion, grief and guilt. Parents may want to withdraw from the outside world, or they may find themselves involved in sudden bursts of activity.

The third stage is a gradual realization that you are able to accept memories without overwhelming grief and you are able to begin forming plans for your future. Decisions become easier to make and practical problems are more easily dealt with.

These stages do vary with each individual and it is impossible to put a time-scale on them. The very fact that they do vary can create pressures for a couple grieving the loss of their child. If one partner is still in the first stage of numbness and disbelief and the other is experiencing overwhelming feelings of anger and despair their emotions and reactions are at odds. They find it difficult to express what they are feeling for fear of hurting one another, and this at a time when each most needs the support of the other. During these times it may help if both partners have another listener outside the immediate family circle to whom they can voice the feelings they are experiencing.

SOME ADVICE FOR HELPERS

It is not easy for parents to start rebuilding their lives after the death of their child. Relatives and friends who offered support in the beginning may drift away, thinking that the worst is over. And the parents are left feeling isolated and depressed because they are still mourning their loss. Often when they need to talk about their child and the way they feel others turn away, embarrassed to talk about the dead.

There are some Do's and Don'ts drawn up by the Compassionate Friends which may help those who know bereaved parents.

They suggest that you let your concern and caring show and that you are *available* — to listen, run errands, help with the children or whatever else seems needed at the time.

. . . *Do* say you are sorry about what happened to their child and about their pain and allow them to express as much grief as they are feeling at that moment and are willing to share.

. . . *Do* encourage them to be patient with themselves and not to expect too much and allow them to talk about the child they have lost as much and as often as they want to.

. . . *Do* talk about the special qualities of that child and give extra attention to brothers or sisters (they too are hurt and confused and in need of attention which their parents may not be able to give at this time.)

. . . *Do* reassure the parents that they did everything they could, and tell them of everything true and positive about the care given to their child.

. . . *Don't* avoid the parents because you are uncomfortable, (being avoided by friends adds pain to an already intolerably painful experience.)

. . . *Don't* say you know how they feel (have you lost a child?), or tell them what they should feel or do — like saying 'You ought to be feeling better now' or 'You must pull yourself together'.

. . . *Don't* change the subject when they mention their dead child or avoid mentioning their child's name because you are scared to remind them of their pain (they will not have forgotten it.)

. . . *Don't* try to find something positive about the death or suggest they can have another child (it would not replace the one they have lost).

. . . *Don't* make any comments which in any way suggest that the care given to their child at home, in hospital or wherever was inadequate (parents are plagued by feelings of doubt and guilt without any help from their family and friends).

Finally, don't let your own sense of helplessness keep you from reaching out to a bereaved parent. No matter how hard it may seem to you, do remember that what they are going through is so much worse and the knowledge that you do care and are concerned will help them much more than silence.

CARE FROM THE HOSPITAL

Many Cardiac Units are becoming increasingly concerned about providing some form of ongoing support for bereaved parents and make a point of inviting parents back to talk over with staff what happened to their child. Some parents welcome this, as at the time of their child's death, there may be too much numbness and sadness to think about why their child died. Later, however, the questions may start and they need to be answered. For many parents too, the staff who cared for their child may be their last link with him and because of this they may want to go back to the unit. Equally though they need a reason for doing so. Obviously this is a very personal decision but it is important that parents do know the choice exists. If bereaved parents are not aware of this, or have not had contact with the unit since, it may be helpful to contact the Nursing Officer or a member of staff they were close to during their child's time in the unit and ask if a visit can be arranged.

Many families find coming back to discuss their child's illness and death with senior members of the team helpful. The optimum time for this visit varies from family to family and is often around six weeks after the child's death. If you have not heard from the team involved then get in touch.

14 RECOMMENDED READING LIST
Books for children

1 GOING TO THE DOCTOR OR HOSPITAL

(i) *Going to the Doctor* by Althea
Dinosaur Publications, 1980
Suitable for the pre-school age group.
A simple description of a visit to the
doctor.

(ii) *Why am I going to Hospital?* by
Carole Livingston
Angus & Robertson, 1983
Suitable for 5+ age group. A lively
down to earth description of why a
child may go to hospital and the sort of
things that will occur. For example,
X-ray, blood tests etc.

(iii) *Zozo goes to Hospital* by Margaret
& Y A Rey
Chatto & Windus, 1978
Pre-school age group for a visit to
hospital.

(iv) *Topsy and Tim go to Hospital* by
Jean & Varety Adamson
School and pre-school age. A visit to
hospital

(v) *Spot's Hospital Visit* by Eric Hall
William Heinemann

(vi) *Emergency Mouse* by Bernard
Stone
Arrow Books, 1981
School and pre-school age.
Anaesthetic, operation and recovery
are covered.

(vii) *Dr Bully Bear* by Peter Bull
Bull and Irving, 1982

(viii) *First Experiences – Going to
Hospital* by Anne Civardi
Usborne

2 ABOUT THE HEART
The Heart for Children
Franklin Watts, 1983
The Heart and Blood Human Body
Series
Suitable for 11+ age group. For older
children who want to understand how
the heart works so that they have a
better idea of their own problem.

3 BEREAVEMENT
(i) *Badgers Parting Gifts* by Susan
Varley
Fontana Picture Book, 1984

(ii) *When Uncle Bob Died* by Althea
Dinosaur Publications, 1982
All very suitable for children and gives
positive angle on death.

(iii) *The Selfish Giant* by Oscar Wilde
Penguin Picture Puffin Series, 1982
A religious story

(iv) *Emma's Cat Dies* by Nigel Snell
Hamish Hamilton, 1984
Designed for small children with lots of
pictures.

(v) *Charlotte's Web* by E B White
Penguin Puffin Books, 1969
Animal story including chapter dealing
with death of the heroine.

(vi) *Watership Down* by Richard Adams
Penguin Puffin Books, 1973
Animal story ending with deaths of the
heroes.

(vii) *Waterbugs and Dragonflies* by
Doris Stickney — published by
Mowbrays

(viii) *I'll always love you* by H. Wilhelm
Knights paperbacks

(ix) *The Velveteen Rabbit*
by M. Williams
Mammoth Books

(x) *A Summer to Die* by L. Lowry
Dragon
An adolescent facing loss for the first
time – death of sister

Books for adults

1 GENERAL
Surgery and your Heart by D Ross & B
Hyams
Beaconsfield Publishers 1982
This book was written for the layman
in order that the patient or parents, the
family and the medical team can come
together on common ground.

Support Services
A Guide to Grants for Individuals in
Need by L Fitzherbert & H Bellafatto
Bath Press, 1987
(Available in any good Ref. Library).
This lists more than 100 charities
under different headings with
descriptions of types of grants given
and to whom. Some are listed
specifically to help sick children and
their families.

Choosing for Children by Priscilla
Alderson
Oxford University Press, 1990
A book, looking at Cardiac Units from
parents eyes and exploring the area of
informed consent.

The Pill 4th Edition by John Guillebaud
Oxford University Press

2 HEALTH GUIDANCE
(i) *Guide to Healthy Eating*
Exercise, Why Bother?
Do You Take Sugar?
3 excellent booklets on healthy diet.
Published by the Health Education
Authority, Hamilton House, Mabledon
Place, London WC1H 9JX at about 10p
each.

(ii) *The Pregnancy Book*
A very clearly written manual
published by the Health Education
Authority at about 50p, but available
free of charge from maternity units for
first-time mothers.

3 BEREAVEMENT
(i) *The Courage to Grieve* by Judy
Tatelman
Heinemann, 1981
A guide through the emotions of grief.

(ii) *A Grief Observed* by C S Lewis
Faber Paperback, 1981
A personal grief experience.

(iii) *Saying Goodbye to Your Baby* by
Priscilla Alderson
Still Birth and Neonatal Death Society
(Sands) Argyle House, 29-31 Euston
Road, London, NW1 2SD

(iv) *Helping Children cope with Grief*
by Rosemary Wells
Sheldon Press

(v) *When People Die* by Williams &
Ross
Macdonald
'why do people die?' – 'what is death?'
– 'facing loss' – 'helping others' –
'beliefs and rituals' – 'no easy answers'
etc

15 SUPPORT GROUPS

Heart Line has available information on many useful organisations. Please contact our Administrator at the following address:

Heart Line Association
c/o
Sun Microsystems Ltd
Watchmoor Park
Camberley
Surrey
Telephone: 0276 416488

Here are some of the major organisations which may be able to help you.

1 **Contact a Family**. This brings together families of handicapped children. They provide support groups and also information about resources all over Britain.
Address – 16 Strutton Ground, London SW1P 2HP. Telephone: 071 222 2695.

2 **Action for Sick Children (formerly 'NAWCH')** are very active in improving conditions in hospital for children and their families. They publish a newsletter and provide a lot of information.
Address – Argyle House, 29-31 Euston Road, London NW1 2SD. Telephone: 071 833 2041.

3 **TAMBA** Twins and Multiple Birth Association.
Address – Gina Siddons, PO Box 30, Little Sutton, L66 1TH. Telephone: 051 348 0200.

4 **Downs Syndrome Association** offers non medical help for parents of Down's Syndrome children, including leaflets and self help branches throughout the UK.
Address – 155 Mitcham Road, London SW17 9PQ. Telephone: 081 682 4001.

5 **The Compassionate Friends** provide support and help for people suffering the loss of a child by others who have been similarly bereaved. There are over 60 groups who meet throughout the British Isles. They have a telephone network and supply leaflets.
Address – 6 Denmark Street, Bristol BS1 5DQ. Telephone: 0272 292778.

6 **Marfan Association** gives information on this condition.
Address – 6 Queens Road, Farnborough, Hants GU14 6DH. Telephone: 0252 547441 and 0252 617320.

7 **National Childbirth Trust**.
Address – Alexandra House, Oldham Terrace, Acton, London W1 6NH. Telephone: 081 992 8637.

8 **The Family Fund**. See page 77 for more information.
Address – PO Box 50, York YO1 22X. Telephone: 0904 621115.

9 **Noonan's Syndrome Society**.
Address – 27 Pinfold Lane, Cheslyn Hay, Walsall, Staffs WS6 7HP. Telephone: 0922 415500 (9.30 am-2.30 pm Monday to Friday).

10 **The British Heart Foundation**.
Address – 14 Fitzhardinge Street, London W1H 9PL. Telephone: 071 935 0185.

ADDRESSES OF CHILDRENS' HEART SUPPORT GROUPS IN THE UK

HEART LINE ASSOCIATION
Chairman: Adrian Gibson,
42 Pevensey Way, Frimley,
Surrey GU16 5YJ.
Telephone: 0252 836609

ASSOCIATION OF CHILDREN
WITH HEART DISORDERS
Chairman: Ian Clegg,
35 Upper Bank End Road, Holmfirth,
Huddersfield, W. Yorks HP7 1EP.
Telephone: 0484 685431

BRISTOL AND SOUTH WEST
CHILDREN'S HEART CIRCLE
Secretary: Mrs Jean Pratten,
19 Coldharbour Road, Redland,
Bristol BS6 7JT.
Telephone: 0272 734373

CHILDREN'S HEART CIRCLE IN
WALES
Secretary: Mrs Margaret Bennett,
27 Brynteg, Rhiwbina,
Cardiff CF4 6TT.
Telephone: 0222 628249

CHUF (Newcastle area)
Secretary: Les Heslop,
28 Diamond Street, Wallsend,
Newcastle on Tyne NE28 8RX.
Telephone: 091 262 6528

DOWNS HEART GROUP
Chairman: Euan Forsythe,
9 Jubilee Drive, Thornbury, Bristol,
Avon BS12 2YG.
Telephone: 0454 413237

ECHO (Guys Hospital London)
Chairman: Chris Goodwin,
144 Stapleton Road, Orpington,
Kent BR6 9TR.
Telephone: 0689 890665

HEARTBEAT
Chairman: Lyn Johnston,
37 Marlborough Crescent, Carryduff,
Co. Down.
Telephone:0232 812935

HEART CARE
Federation of Childrens' Heart Support
Groups.
Telephone: 0396 614206

HEART LINK
Chairman: Glenis Barnes,
83 Meadowbrook Road,
Kibworth Beauchamp,
Leicester LE8 OH6.
Telephone: 0533 792006

WESSEX CHILDREN'S HEART
CIRCLE
Chairman: Mrs Angela Coxon,
48 South Avenue, Sherborne,
Dorset DT9 6AP.
Telephone: 0935 816156

YOUNG AT HEART (West Midlands)
Chairman: R Hickinbotham,
5 Orchard Close, Handsworth,
Birmingham B21 9PH.
Telephone: 021 523 7840

You may find local branches of these organisations listed on the 'Helplines' page at the front of The Thomson Directory.

16 MEDICAL TERMS – A dictionary for Parents

Medical terms are often very confusing. Many of those that are frequently used in relation to children with heart problems are listed here with a brief explanation. If there are any others related to your child that are used and you do not understand, please ask members on the team involved in your child's care to explain.

ABDOMEN — tummy

ABSCESS — a localized collection of infected liquid called pus.

ACIDOSIS — loss of the normal balance of body chemistry resulting from poor heart action and poor blood supply to parts of the body.

ANAEMIA — reduction in the red blood cell count.

ANAESTHETIC — a chemical that produces loss of consciousness.

ANALGESIC — a chemical substance that produces freedom from pain.

ANEURYSM — a ballooning of the wall of a blood vessel or of the heart.

ANGIOPLASTY — stretching of a narrow artery by a balloon catheter.

ANOMALOUS — wrong.

ANTICOAGULANT — a drug used to reduce blood clotting.

AORTA — main artery from the heart to the body.

AORTIC ARCH — topmost part of the aorta from which the head, neck and arm arteries arise.

AORTIC VALVE — the valve between the main pumping chamber and the aorta.

ARRHYTHMIA — irregular or abnormal heart action.

ARTERY — a blood vessel that carries blood away from the heart.

ASCITES — fluid in the abdomen.

ASYSTOLE — stoppage of heart action.

ATHEROMA — damage to the lining of arteries producing narrowing and reduction of blood flow onto which clots may form.

ATRESIA — blocked/missing/never formed.

ATRIUM — receiving chamber of heart.

AUTOPSY — examination of the body after death.

BANDING — an artificial narrowing of the lung artery with a 'band' or string to reduce blood flow.

BIFURCATION — division into two.

BIOPSY — removal of a small piece of tissue.

BLOOD PRESSURE — the pressure of blood within the vessels.

BRADYCARDIA — slow heart rate.

BRONCHUS — main airway to each lung.

CAPILLARIES — very fine blood vessels through whose walls food, oxygen, waste products, carbon dioxide are filtered to and from the body tissues.

CARBON DIOXIDE — waste gas produced as a by-product of body activity.

CARDIAC — heart.

CARDIAC OUTPUT — the amount of blood pumped by the heart per minute.

CARDIOMYOPATHY — disease of heart muscle.

CARDIOPLEGIA — a chemical solution used to protect heart muscle during open heart surgery.

CARDIOPULMONARY BYPASS — a machine with a pump and an oxygenator to maintain blood supply to the body while the heart's action is stopped.

CATHETER — fine plastic tube to measure pressures or drain fluid.

CEREBRO-VASCULAR ACCIDENT — see stroke

CHOLESTEROL — a fatty chemical found particularly in animal fat.

CHORDAE TENDINAE — fibrous cords that support the mitral and tricuspid valves.

CHOREA — spontaneous abnormal purposeless movements.

CHROMOSOMES — the basic protein that characterizes each individual.

CHYLE — a fluid containing a lot of fat contained within the lymphatic system.

CLUBBING — rounded swelling of the ends of the fingers or toes.

COARCTATION — narrowing in a blood vessel.

COLLATERALS — natural additional blood vessels to help overcome a blockage.

CONDUIT — artificial tube.

CONGENITAL — present at birth.

CONGESTION — too much fluid in a part of the body.

CONSOLIDATION — part of lungs becoming airless.

CONVULSION — a fit.

CORONARY ARTERIES — the blood supply to the heart muscle.

CORONER — an official who inquires into unnatural death eg, sudden, unexpected or those related to procedures or operations.

CORRECTIVE — to return the circulation to normal.

CPAP — constant positive airway pressure, a way of keeping small airspaces open.

CYANOSIS — blue colouration of skin and lips owing to a lower amount of oxygen in the capillaries.

DEFIBRILLATOR — a machine to give an electrical shock used to treat abnormalities of heart rhythm.

DIALYSIS — a method of washing out waste products.

DIAPHRAGM — important muscle of breathing that separates the chest from the abdomen.

DIASTOLE — resting phase of heart action.

DIASTOLIC BLOOD PRESSURE — the lower of the blood pressure readings.

DOPPLER — the use of sound waves to assess speed and direction of blood flow.

DRAIN — a tube used to move fluid or air from the body.

DRIP — a means of getting food and drugs into a vein.

DUCT — a tube carrying fluid or blood.

DYSPHAGIA — difficulty with swallowing.

DYSPNOEA — breathlessness.

ECHOCARDIOGRAM — a picture of the heart and blood vessels using reflected high frequency sound waves.

-ECTOMY — removal.

ELECTROCARDIOGRAM — recording of the electrical activity of the heart.

ELECTRODES — fine wires that carry electrical activity from or into the heart.

EMBOLUS — an abnormal substance within the blood stream such as clot or air.

EMBRYO — the developing baby within the womb.

ENDOCARDIUM — smooth lining on the inside of the heart and its valves.

FAILURE — inability of the organ to cope with demands.

FALLOT'S TETRALOGY — combination of a hole between the ventricles, obstruction of blood flow to the lungs and a displacement of the aorta.

FAMILIAL — runs in families.

FEMORAL — related to the leg.

FIBRILLATION — disorganised heart contractions.

FLUTTER — abnormally fast regular beating usually of the atria.

FETUS sometimes spelt 'foetus' — developing baby within the womb.

FORAMEN OVALE — small hole between the two receiving chambers.

GENE — an inherited characteristic, a part of a chromosome.

HAEMATOMA — a localized collection of blood outside a vessel.

HAEMOGLOBIN — the chemical carried in red cells that carries oxygen, carbon dioxide and gives colour to the blood.

HAEMOLYSIS — destruction of red cells.

HAEMOPTYSIS — blood coughed up from lungs.

HAEMORRHAGE — a leak of blood from blood vessels.

HEART BLOCK — a disturbance in the rhythm of the heart so that the ventricles beat slower than the atria.

HEART LUNG MACHINE — a machine that oxygenates and pumps blood around the body while heart operations are carried out.

HETEROGRAFT (also called XENOGRAFT) — using a tissue from another species.

HOMOGRAFT (also called ALLOGRAFT) — using tissue from another human.

HYPER — too much.

HYPERTENSION — elevated blood pressure.

HYPERTHERMIA — very high temperature.

HYPO — too little.

HYPOTENSION — low blood pressure.

HYPOTHERMIA — very low temperature.

IDIOPATHIC — cause unknown.

IMMUNIZATION — a method of increasing patient's defence against infection.

INCOMPETENCE — leaking.

INFANT — less than one year.

INFARCT — death of tissue related to blocking of the blood supply.

INFRA — below.

INFUSION — fluid or medication given slowly into a vein.

INTRA — within.

INTUBATION — passage of a tube into the windpipe to assist with breathing.

ISCHAEMIA — reduction in organ function as a result of reduced blood supply.

-ITIS — infection.

JAUNDICE — yellow colouring of skin and eyes as a result of liver dysfunction or red cell breakdown.

JUXTA — nearby.

KELOID — a hard, lumpy scar from excess fibrous tissue.

LEUCOCYTE — white blood cell that fights infection.

LOBE — part of an organ.
LYMPH — body fluid running in channels, drains fluid and particularly fats from the bowel back into the circulation.

MEDIASTINUM — space in the chest between the lungs, heart and great vessels.
MITRAL VALVE — two-cusped valve between the left atrium and left ventricle.
MONOCUSP — using a single cusp from a donor valve.
MURMUR — noise produced by blood flow in the heart and vessels.

NEONATE — baby in the first month of life.
NODE — area of specialized cell that controls the rhythm of the heart.
NUCLEUS — central part of most cells and contains the chromosomes.

OEDEMA — extra fluid accumulating in the tissue.
OESOPHAGUS — gullet
OLIGURIA — too little urine.
-OLOGY — the study of.
-OSTOMY — a hole.
-OTOMY — an incision.
OXIMETER — a machine to measure oxygen.
OXYGEN — part of the air that is needed by all animal cells for normal working.
OXYGENATOR — an artificial machine that delivers oxygen into the blood.

PACEMAKER — electrical control of the heart — natural/artificial.
PACING WIRES — wires that connect an artificial pacemaker to the heart.

PALLIATION — a procedure to improve the patient's condition.
PALPITATION — an uncomfortable sensation of heart beat which may be slow, fast, irregular or regular.
PARASYMPATHETIC NERVES — nerves to the heart that slow heart rate.
PARENTERAL — medicines given by injection.
PEDIATRIC sometimes spelt 'paediatric' — word to describe science of medical problems in children.
-PARESIS — paralysis.
PERI — nearby.
PERICARDIUM — lining bag in which the heart sits.
PERITONEUM — membrane lining the inside of the abdomen.
PHRENIC NERVE — nerve that supplies the diaphragm.
PHYSIOLOGICAL — functioning normally.
PLACENTA — part of the uterus that supplies the developing baby with nourishment and removes waste products.
PLASMA — liquid part of the blood.
PLATELETS — small particles in the blood which are important for blood clotting.
PLEURA — covering layer of the lungs and the inside of the chest.
PNEUMOTHORAX — air outside the lung and within the chest cavity.
POLYCYTHAEMIA — increased number of red blood cells.
PRECORDIUM — part of the chest in front of the heart.
PROGNOSIS — an estimation of outlook for the patients particular problem.
PROPHYLAXIS — prevention.
PROSTHETIC — artificial.
PULMONARY — the adjective used to describe lungs.

PULMONARY VALVE — the valve between the right ventricle and the lung artery.

PULSE — the arterial beat from forward blood flow produced by the heart contraction.

PUS — liquid produced by infection.

PYREXIA — high temperature.

RADIOGRAPH — photograph of part of the body using X-rays.

RADIO-ISOTOPE — a substance that gives off a small dose of radioactivity. It is used for diagnostic purposes.

REGURGITANT — backward flow, leaking.

RENAL — pertaining to kidneys.

RESUSCITATION — a general term used to encompass treatment when the patient is very ill.

SAC — bag.

SALINE — salt solution usually the same strength as body fluid.

SAPHENOUS — a vein in the leg.

SCLEROSIS — hardening of tissue.

SCOLIOSIS — curvature of the spine.

SEMILUNAR — crescent shaped, relates to the aortic or pulmonary valve leaflets.

SEPTECTOMY — removal of a septum.

SEPTICAEMIA — an infection of the blood stream.

SEPTOSTOMY — a hole in the septum.

SEPTUM — a dividing structure.

SHOCK — severe failure of the circulation with cessation of normal body action.

SHUNT — a natural or artificial tube used to increase blood supply to the lungs.

SIGN — an abnormality found on examination.

SPHYGMOMANOMETER — instrument for measuring blood pressure.

STENOSIS — narrowing in the vessel or valve.

STERNUM — breast bone.

STRIDOR — noisy breathing.

STROKE — loss of brain function related to blockage or bursting of its supplying blood vessel.

SUB — below.

SUBCLAVIAN — below the clavicle.

SUPRA — above.

SUTURE — fine string used to sew two parts together.

SYMPATHETIC NERVE — nerves to the heart that increase the heart rate.

SYMPTOM — complaint described by patient or family.

SYNCOPE — loss of consciousness related to lack of blood flow to the brain.

SYNDROME — a collection of abnormalities that together produce a recognisable pattern.

SYSTOLE — the period of contraction of the pumping chambers.

SYSTOLIC BLOOD PRESSURE — the top of blood pressure measurement taken when the heart is contracting.

TACHYCARDIA — rapid heart rate.

TACHYPNOEA — rapid breathing.

TAMPONADE — obstruction to filling of the heart by pressure from a surrounding collection of fluid.

THORACIC DUCT — vessel carrying lymph drainage from bowel through the chest to the subclavian vein.

THORACOTOMY — an operation on the chest.

THRESHOLD — lowest level of stimulus that will produce a response.

THRILL — vibration that can be felt, produced by abnormal blood flow.

THROMBOLYSIS — dissolving a clot in a blood vessel with drugs.

THROMBOSIS — clot formation.

THROMBUS — clot.

TOXIC — an illness related to a poisonous by-product usually infection.

TRACHEA — windpipe.

TRACHEOMALACIA — softening of the cartilage that supports the windpipe.

TRACHEOSTOMY — a small tube through a hole in the windpipe to assist ventilation.

TRANSPLANT — replace an organ by one from another person.

TRANSPOSITION — a change in the connection of chambers or blood vessels.

TRICUSPID VALVE — three leaflet valve between the right atrium and right ventricle.

TRUNCUS — single vessel arising from the heart that divides into aorta and lung artery.

UMBILICAL — tube that connects the placenta to the developing baby.

VACCINATION — used generally for immunization.

VACCINE — a liquid of weak or killed micro-organisms, or their proteins that can be used to prevent diseases.

VAGUS NERVE — nerve supply to the body and bowel, stimulation of which slows the heart rate.

VALVE — structure which allows blood flow in one direction and prevents leakage.

VALVOPLASTY — stretching of a narrow valve often with a balloon catheter.

VALVOTOMY — cutting or stretching of a narrow valve.

VASCULAR — relating to blood vessels.

VEGETATION — lumpy areas on heart valve caused by infection and blood clot.

VEIN (VENA) — thin walled vessel carrying blood towards the heart.

VENTRICLE — pumping chamber of heart.

You may find it helpful for your consultant to use these pages to explain your child's heart condition.

YOUR CHILD'S HEART

You may find it helpful for your consultant to use these pages to explain your child's heart condition.

YOUR CHILD'S HEART AFTER OPERATION

QUESTIONS
FOR MY CHILD'S
DOCTORS